DAVID BOON'S
FUNNIEST
SPORTING
MOMENTS

DAVID BOON'S
FUNNIEST SPORTING MOMENTS

HILARIOUS MISHAPS
AND MOMENTS FROM OUR
FAVOURITE SPORTS

DAVID BOON
with Eamon Evans

ALLEN&UNWIN
SYDNEY · MELBOURNE · AUCKLAND · LONDON

First published in 2012

Copyright © David Boon 2012

Allen & Unwin
Sydney, Melbourne, Auckland, London

83 Alexander Street
Crows Nest NSW 2065
Australia
Phone: (61 2) 8425 0100
Fax: (61 2) 9906 2218
Email: info@allenandunwin.com
Web: www.allenandunwin.com

Cataloguing-in-Publication details are available
from the National Library of Australia
www.trove.nla.gov.au

ISBN 978 1 74331 324 4

Internal design and illustration by Squirt Creative
Set in 11/15 pt Gill Sans Book by Bookhouse, Sydney
Printed and bound in Australia by the SOS Print + Media Group.

10 9 8 7 6 5 4 3

MIX
Paper from
responsible sources
FSC® C011217

The paper in this book is FSC® certified.
FSC® promotes environmentally responsible,
socially beneficial and economically viable
management of the world's forests.

CONTENTS

CONTENTS

FOREWORD

I was privileged to have played cricket for Australia at an international level for a long time, travelling the world playing the game that I love.

Having the opportunity to meet people and characters from all walks of life and nationalities was amazing. These opportunities were not just restricted to cricket and along the way relationships were born with many people, both in other sports and various entertainment industries.

The yarns you hear and the experiences you have, provide countless stories and anecdotes related by the least obvious sources in many cases. Watching sporting events, a conversation while having a quiet one, you would never know when the prospect would arise. Mind you with some, the principal of 'never let the truth get in the way of a good story' may or may not apply. I will let you be the judge.

At first I thought it would be a chore to remember these moments and dig out all those stories which have become legend. However, it turned out to be a fun project getting together with Eamon Evans to gather the best of the best.

I thank Allen and Unwin, our publishers, for approaching me to do so.

I hope you enjoy reading this book as much as I did reminiscing over some good old classic tales as well as some new ones, albeit some are a bit risqué.

David Boon

CRICKET
MOMENTS

*Cricket is the only game that you can
actually put on weight while playing.*

Tommy Docherty

An early Christmas present

The West Indies pace attack of the 1980s was a fearsome sight to behold. Curtly Ambrose could be particularly unsettling: six feet, seven inches of pure athleticism, he was, as Ian Botham put it, 'a cricketer who thrived on aggression and menace'.

When he was dressed in pads and a helmet, Geoff Lawson was a less fearsome sight to behold. Like many bowlers before and after him, Geoff never quite got the hang of life at the other end of the crease. Give him expert training and a state-of-the-art cricket bat, and he'd still find a way to defend with his face.

Or that's what happened at the 1989 Perth Test, anyway: Big Curtly bowled a bouncer, and broke Geoff's jaw in five different places.

Lawson later recalled that his team mates were very supportive while he recuperated over the next few days. Merv Hughes even brought him a gift. 'I was quite touched. What a nice thought from the big, ugly bugger. An early Christmas present to ease my pain.

'I ripped the parcel open, hoping for a book or maybe even a video. No, nothing like that. A box of spearmint chewing gum!'

Hawke talk

Former PM Bob Hawke loves his cricket, even though cricket didn't always love him. In 1984, the one-time first class cricketer famously headed up a team of politicians in a match against the Parliamentary Press Gallery. He made a quick-fire 28, smashing the ball all over the ground—and then top-edged a hook and managed to smash up his face. Glasses broken and ego shattered, Hawkie was forced to retire hurt but he eventually returned to the field and led his team to a glorious victory.

Three years later, he was at it again, lining up at the MCG against the Melbourne Crusaders—another pack of hacks. The PM was making mincemeat of the bowling, until he belted one straight to journalist Ken Piesse at wide long-on.

Trudging back to the boundary, Hawkie was heard to mutter: 'First time I've been caught out by a journo in 25 years.'

Negotiating the seed

With flirting techniques, results may vary: one person's come-on is another's turn-off. Sledging is a bit the same. What Steve Waugh used to call 'mental disintegration' often does just that to a batsman, causing him to lose his concentration—or, better yet, his self-esteem. But other batsmen simply get fired up. Sledging *them* is a bit like coming across a beehive and deciding to give it a bit of a shake.

Viv Richards was one such batsman. The Master Blaster was a bad man to provoke. But in a 1986 game at Somerset Cricket Ground, set on the banks of the River Tone at Taunton, Greg Thomas of Glamorgan nonetheless decided to give it a try.

'Viv, it's red and round. Can't you see it?' teased the up-and-coming quickie after he'd manage to whizz one past the bat.

It was the same story next ball. 'Viv, you seem to be having a little trouble negotiating the seed today. For your information, it's red, it's round, and it weighs five-and-a-half ounces.'

Ball three, however, did not reach the keeper—Big Viv hit it into the river. 'As you know what it bleeding well looks like, you had better go find it,' the great man replied.

Pentridge people

Everyone who's ever played sport knows the frustration of losing a ball (insert Lance Armstrong joke here.) Golf is famously prone to the problem, of course, but it's an even bigger issue in Major League baseball, where spectators are allowed to keep everything that the batter hits into the crowd. It's estimated that between 60 and 70 balls are used each game.

In professional cricket, a lost ball is much rarer. One of the first times it happened in Australia was around the time of the First World War. Coburg faced Brighton in a district match at Coburg Cricket Club, and Gordon Robinson, a big bloke at six foot and twelve-and-a-half stone, was at the crease.

Big Gordon could produce some big shots and he hit seven sixes while he was at bat. One of those impressive shots soared over the wall of Pentridge Prison—it never came back.

It was one of the jokes of the players at the time that it shows you what sort of people are in Pentridge these days.

When our prime minister
got the boot

Some Australians like to think that our storied cricket rivalry against the 'old enemy'—England, of course—isn't really a rivalry at all. Just big wins followed by narrow wins, with some medium-sized wins here and there. Occasional losses are chalked down to overconfidence, or some blunder on the selectors' part.

Unfortunately, the record doesn't quite bear that out: England has won the Ashes plenty of times, most recently in 2011.

Australian prime ministers have sometimes struggled in England too. When England won the Ashes in 2009, former PM John Howard was delivering a speech at Cambridge University when one of the students took exception to his presence.

'He was Australian and he shouted, "Go home racist",' recalled an observer, 'and then he got up and threw a shoe. It was the weakest throw in the world. I mean, it shows why you lost the Ashes, if you don't mind me saying.'

2.06 metres of fury

There may be no fool like an old fool, as the saying goes—and, who knows, it might be true.

One thing we can say for certain, however, is that there's no tool like a young tool. Patrick Patterson provides a case in point. Famous for threatening to kill batsmen—and then actually trying to—Patto had what you might call a fast bowler's temperament. During the Adelaide Test in 1989, however, this temperament was put to the test. The 28-year-old West Indian player spent the whole day hurling thunderbolts, only to see Merv Hughes—of *all* people—make an unbeaten 72.

At the end of the day's play, a small 81-year-old named Donald Bradman visited the West Indies dressing room, and all the players immediately stood in a show of respect. All, that is, except the fuming Patterson. He stormed over to Bradman, 2.06 metres of fury, and spat, 'You, Don Bradman? You, Don Bradman? I kill you, man! I bowl at you, I kill you! I split you in two!'

'You couldn't even get Merv Hughes out,' Bradman replied. 'You'd have no chance against me, mate!'

Howzaaaaaat?

What's the worst thing that can happen to a cricket umpire? His guide dog bites him—boom tish!

The second worst thing, of course, is having to hear jokes like that. Umpiring is an impossibly difficult profession: standing stock still for five solid days, eyes glued to the stumps, all so you can judge what might or might not have happened in the course of half a split second. Snicko, Hawk-Eye, commentators, the crowd and several hundred journalists will let you know if you've made the wrong decision, and if you've made the right one, you're just doing your job.

In the 1970s, an umpire who made the wrong decision would also get to hear from BS Chandrasekhar. A leg-spinner known for his dislike of poor decisions, the Indian player once appealed for LBW on four consecutive balls. Each was given 'not out', even though the last one, at least, was plumb.

Finally, on the last ball of the over, BS slipped in a googly and managed to clean bowl the batsman. He excitedly turned to the Australian umpire and gave a loud cry of 'Howzaaaaat?'

The umpire looked confused. 'He's bowled,' he said.

'I know he's bowled, but is he out?'

A special meal

A trip to India is good for the soul but the stomach can often suffer. Travellers to India frequently fall victim to Delhi belly, a condition that, for cricketers, means a less desirable type of runs. Some cricketers therefore choose to skip local cuisine. In 1998, Heinz rushed a crate of baked beans and tinned spaghetti to the Australian spinner Shane Warne after he stated to the media that he was 'really craving some canned spaghetti on toast'.

Alec Stewart also liked to play it safe. On England's 2006 tour of the subcontinent, five players went down with gastro, but that wicketkeeper came prepared. Stewart took with him 43 separate portions of his favourite meal: chicken with mashed potato and broccoli. By eating it for dinner every night, he managed to get through the tour without a single wet fart—although he did get sick of that particular meal.

After many weeks on tour, Stewart arrived home in England to find that his wife had prepared a special meal to welcome him home—a huge helping of chicken, mashed potato and broccoli.

The bunny and the tummy

One of the great things about being a cricket player is that you don't need to get too obsessive about the gym. While footballers and tennis players and Olympians are forever working on their quads and pecs and glutes, a cricketer can pretty much ignore his body unless he wants to fill it with pizza and beer.

Every now and then, though, a cricketer can have a few too many pizzas, and wash them down with too many beers. When Shane Warne waddled out to play South Africa in the 1997 Boxing Day Test, he wasn't quite as streamlined as he'd been in years past. The spinner's competitive spirit was still in good shape, however: 'I've waited two years for another chance to humiliate you,' he growled at his 'bunny', the batsman Daryll Cullinan.

The bunny looked Warne up and down. 'Looks like you spent it eating.'

The cherished elder

When the Don died, the nation mourned. More than 50 years after his final match, millions tuned into Bradman's funeral to hear the Governor-General pay tribute to 'a cherished elder of our nation . . . the best known and most admired Australian of our times'.

As the greatest cricketer of all time, there's no doubt the Don was admired. 'As the years passed, his public stature continued to grow,' David Frith once wrote, 'until the sense of reverence and unquestioning worship left many of his contemporaries scratching their heads in wondering admiration.' Stadiums, museums, parks and roads have all been named after the great man. Even in his 80s, he spent up to three hours a day answering letters from adoring fans.

For his son, all this adulation can sometimes get a bit much. 'I was in the State Library recently, where some of his things are in a collection,' John Bradman once said. 'One of the items is a rug which used to be on the floor of my room. It's in the design of the Australian blazer pocket and it has a dark green background and in this dark green background are some faded patches.

'I was standing next to some people and they were discussing these pale patches in hushed tones and with almost reverential significance . . . I could have told them they were the patches where my little dog had peed.'

Cultural differences

Viv Richards was a frightening man. 'His very strut to the wicket intimidated even the most certain of bowlers,' a journalist recently recalled. 'By the time he had taken guard, then fixed them with an eye, many were already quivering wrecks.'

'He had an aura given to no other,' agrees former England medium pacer, Mike Selvey. 'Truly he was scary . . . [When he looked] down his aquiline nose to eyeball the bowler, it was almost as if he was sniffing the air . . . for the scent of fear.'

But some bowlers don't scare easy. When big Merv Hughes bowled to the Master Blaster, he decided to eyeball him right back. Pretty much every delivery Merv sent down during that tour of the Caribbean was followed up with a lingering stare.

'This is my island, my culture,' Viv eventually said, irritated. 'Don't you be staring at me. In my culture we just bowl.'

Merv said nothing—until he bowled Viv out. 'In my culture, we just say piss off.'

Ticket, please

Apart from sex and beer and curry and the Beatles and, well, one or two dozen other things, nothing beats the first day of an Ashes Test. But it just isn't the same if you miss the first ball.

At one time—according to former England batsman Mike Gatting—the retired English middle-distance runner Sebastian Coe was in danger of doing just that. He'd raced right up to the WG Grace Memorial Gates at Lord's, only to be informed that his ticket was for entry through the North Gate, all the way over on the other side of the ground.

'Please let me in here or else I'll miss the first ball.'

'No, sir.'

'Do you know who I am?'

'No, sir.'

'I am Sebastian Coe, the Olympic gold medallist and world record breaker in the 800 metres, 1500 metres and the mile.'

'Oh. Well in that case it shouldn't take you too long to run round to the North Gate.'

Talking about walking

To walk or not to walk, that is the question.

Most cricketers answer 'Hell, no!' While Adam Gilchrist famously gave himself out at the 2003 World Cup—walking away from the crease because he knew he'd snicked the ball, even though the umpire hadn't raised a finger—most batsmen manage to keep their honesty at bay. You're often given out when you're not, goes their logic, so why not stay in when you're out?

The Reverend David Sheppard disagreed. While the Lord was his shepherd, David certainly wasn't a sheep. A fierce enemy of Apartheid who had the courage to speak out against the Falklands War, Sheppard also trod his own path as a county cricketer—or, rather, he chose to walk.

Sheppard walked so often, in fact, that he managed to infuriate his team mates at Sussex. Eventually, they asked their captain, Robin Marlar, if he could have a quiet word. Sternly, Marlar told Sheppard that he was in the team to bat, not to preach. The team was sick of losing just because he chose to take some kind of ethical stand.

The good reverend reacted with fury. 'What! You want me to cheat at cricket and stay in when I know I'm out?' he shouted. 'Why, I'd rather commit adultery.'

'Well, who wouldn't?' replied Marlar quite reasonably.

The all-rounder

The legendary cricketer WG Grace was once asked for his thoughts on what makes a good batsman. 'I should like to say that good batsmen are born, not made,' the great man replied, 'but my long experience comes up before me, and tells me that it is not so.'

Merv Hughes certainly wasn't born a good batsman— you didn't need much experience to see *that*—but for a time there it looked like he might make one. In a 1989 Test at the Adelaide Oval, the fast bowler came out to bat in his customary position of number 10. Dean Jones, his partner at the batting crease, was tantalisingly close to a double century, and must have felt a bit like a general cursed with really bad troops. 'Don't worry about your score,' he implored Big Merv. 'Just block everything and try to stay in.'

So Merv naturally started going for his shots. And, rather unnaturally, he started doing it well. 'I got 72 "red inks", the first time I can recall leaving the field with my bat raised,' Hughes later said, 'and when I got back to the rooms, there were all my team mates formed in a congratulatory semicircle.'

The captain, Allan Border, was the first to speak. 'Merv, you could be Australia's leading all-rounder—if you could get some wickets.'

Warwick the weighty

Australian cricketers have always liked to keep in shape. It's just that a lot of the time that shape is a circle.

An all-rounder in more ways than one, Warwick Armstrong was the biggest thing in Australian cricket at the start of the 20th century, both on the field and on the scales. Six foot three and around 140 kilograms, the big bloke smoked, drank and sweated so much that a puddle of perspiration often formed at the crease. And Armstrong's leg spin bowling action, according to *Sporting Life*, was 'rather like a fat uncle', and 'not altogether unlike a fat aunt'.

But boy could the Big Ship play. With a batting average of 56 and 117 wickets at 15.47, Armstrong was an out-and-out champion, a cricketer feared by every opponent and worshipped by every fan.

The story goes that Armstrong once encountered one such fan on a sunny afternoon in Hampshire. A little boy kept hovering beside him, following the Australian captain wherever he went. Ever patient with the hoi polloi, Armstrong kindly turned to him.

'Here, give me your autograph book and I'll sign it.'

'I ain't got one.'

'Then what do you want?'

'Please, sir, you are the only decent bit of shade in the place.'

Classy times at Lord's

Lord's isn't actually named after some member of the aristocracy—its first owner was Thomas Lord, the son of a Yorkshire labourer. But even so, it's often filled with nobs. Being home to the Marylebone Cricket Club (original name: 'The Noblemen's and Gentlemen's Club'), the famous cricket ground hosts many posh functions, which Test players are obliged to attend.

The former Australian off-spinner Ashley Mallet has a great yarn about one such function, which occurred during the Second Ashes Test in 1968. Like all his team mates, he was on his best behaviour, self-consciously sipping tea, nibbling cucumber sandwiches, and trying hard to not break any china.

'I distinctly remember talking among a group of fellow players when I saw from a distance of about ten yards the figure of a rather elegant-looking woman approaching,' Mallet once recalled.

'My short-sightedness had never really embarrassed me before, but I really couldn't make out who the woman was, and called out, "I say my dear, will you not join us here?"

'By now you will have realised that it was none other than Queen Elizabeth.'

A cricket-tragic's wife

Like a few Aussie PMs before and after him, Robert Menzies was a cricket tragic. The founder of the Prime Minister's XI, he was known to schedule official trips to England so that they coincided with an Ashes series. He once even paid for Keith Stackpole to receive a little extra leg spin coaching.

Bob's wife, however, was somewhat less of a fan, as a journalist once found out. 'I've only seen one Test match in Australia, back in 1924,' said Dame Pattie Menzies in answer to his question, late in the 1930s. 'England was playing Australia and my husband suggested I should go at least one day of the match. When I arrived at the ground, Hobbs and Sutcliffe were batting, and after watching them for a couple of hours, I became bored, and went home.'

'And that was the last game you saw?' asked the journalist.

'Oh no, I went to England in 1926, and Bob suggested that I should see at least one match in England. So I went to the Oval where England was again playing Australia, and what do you think? When I arrived at the ground, there they were again, Hobbs and Sutcliffe. They were still batting.'

Sorry, Fred

Life can offer no lonelier feeling than the few moments that follow dropping an easy catch. You just want the earth to swallow you up, chew slowly and spit you out into the fiery sun. The crowd boos, the bowler glares and your team mates avoid your eye. Sometimes you can even overhear your parents in the grandstand, telling the people next to them that you were adopted. That's when a good team mate needs to step in and offer an encouraging word, a pat on the back or a quick, cheerful wink: whatever it takes to boost sagging morale.

Fred Trueman was not a good team mate. The story goes that once, during a county match in the 1950s, that paceman produced an unplayable leg-cutter, that sent an easy knick right to first slip. But the slipper not only managed to miss the catch; the ball flew through his legs for a boundary.

At the change of ends, he sheepishly apologised. 'Sorry, Fred, I should've kept my legs together.'

'Not you, son,' Trueman snarled. 'Your mother should've.'

A leader of men

In cricket, leadership is very important. The best captains are bold and decisive. They set adventurous fields and declare at dangerous times, mix up the batting order, and change bowlers on a whim. They want a result and they go for it, even at the risk of a loss.

Other captains, however, never really take the plunge; they just let games aimlessly drift. This can be particularly annoying when someone's been bowling without success for hours, and a change clearly needs to be made.

In 1928, a Gloucestershire paceman named Tom Goddard was forced to bowl for three hours straight in sweltering, heat-wave conditions. 'Why the hell doesn't the bloody bugger take me off?' he panted to the wicketkeeper at the end of his 42nd consecutive over.

'It's not his fault,' replied the keeper. The captain, he pointed out, had actually left the field with an injury a few hours ago, and left his vice-captain in command.

Tom Goddard stopped complaining—he was the vice-captain.

The glorious baggy green

Once, when he was Australia's prime minister, John Howard stated he actually only had the second most important job in the country. The most important one belonged to Ricky Ponting.

Whether or not Howard had his tongue in his cheek, it's safe to say that Australians take their Test cricket very seriously: kids all over the country dream of one day taking the field. 'The baggy green is revered by everyone with a connection to Australian cricket,' says another former captain, Mark 'Tubby' Taylor. 'Being awarded a baggy green is the ultimate for a cricketer in Australia . . . [It's a] badge of honour appreciated by everyone who loves the game in Australia and abroad.'

All very true, no doubt, but it's worth noting that the chance to represent your country wasn't always so revered. The first paceman selected for Australia's very first Test match in 1877 was a Victorian left-armer named Francis Allan. And he would have been the first man to bowl a ball, had he not declined the invitation to play. So he could go to an agricultural fair in Warrnambool.

The glass eye

While people *do* go to Lord's to watch cricket, their first priority is usually to drink. Watching cricket without beer is like eating cereal without milk: OK, but you work up a thirst. It was during one such drinking-cum-cricket watching session at the Tavern Pub in Lord's that a group of actors hit upon a fine idea: they would form a cricket club to be known as the Lord's Taverners, and play games for charity every year.

For one such game, in 1969, the Taverners recruited a dynamic opening batsman named Colin Milburn. His cricket career had been tragically cut short by a car accident that had cost him his left eye.

And after the third ball, he lost the eye again. A fastish delivery forced him to swerve away, and Milburn's glass eye fell out of its socket. The batsman nonchalantly bent down, picked it up and put it back in its place.

'Good God! Did you see that?' exclaimed the horrified umpire.

'Ah yes,' replied a nearby Taverner. 'Milburn always takes three balls to get his eye in.'

Captain Grumpy

Allan Border's nickname was Captain Grumpy and on the whole it was well deserved. While a lot of sports captains these days tend to be SNAGs first, sportsmen second—sensitive and supportive among team mates, and always ready to accommodate an opponent—AB was a bit more old school. 'What do you think this is, a tea party?' he once asked a thirsty English batsman. 'No, you can't have a glass of water. You can bloody well wait like all the rest of us.'

An Aussie bowler named Dave Gilbert received an equal amount of warmth and tenderness during a one-day international in 1986. At one point while he was bowling, a Pakistani batsman dabbed a ball to cover and took off. 'AB swooped, turned and threw at my end,' Gilbert later recalled. 'I tried to reposition myself for the throw but it struck me in the middle of the back at top pace.' Ouch.

Strangely enough, the exact same thing happened next ball: 'The same shot, the same throw, and then "whack" in the back.

'I was in agony and AB burst out with, "For God's sake, Lizard, get out of the bloody way!"'

A nervous debut

Is there anything more nerve-racking than making your Test debut? Players spend their whole boyhood dreaming about the baggy green. They practise hour after hour, day after day, just for the chance to represent their country and hear that big roar from the crowd. Then suddenly there they are, right alongside their heroes. Players they only know from the poster that had pride of place on their bedroom wall.

Pity, then, poor John Benaud, a right-hand batsman for NSW. The much younger brother of Richie, he played three Tests for Australia, and will forever wince when he remembers the first. 'In a nervous moment, I lit a cigarette and carelessly waved out the match,' he once recalled of the game against Pakistan at the Adelaide Oval.

'Like the arrow in the air, it fell I know not where— until Dennis Lillee began shouting that his cricket bat was on fire. He was wrong, it was only his shirt and trousers.'

Dear Sir Fred

Like art and music and children's television, cricket can be appreciated on many different levels. The people who like it the most tend to be the ones with strong and detailed opinions about technique. What makes a good off-drive or great late cut? Where should one pitch a googly? When's the right time for a flipper?

Sir Fred Trueman was one such aficionado. A champion bowler turned outspoken radio commentator, his deliveries involved a fluid, side-on action that was straight out of the textbook— and he maintained that everyone else should bowl the same way. The proper batting stance was also side-on, said Fred. He was a stickler for turning sideways.

And it appeared that his message was getting through. One day on radio, his fellow commentators read out the following letter from a listener:

Dear Sir Fred
Let me first say that I am your greatest fan. You have been a stellar performer for England and now as a commentator you continue to spread the knowledge of the game.

Sir, I would want to say that based on your recent comments I have changed my stance to side-on hoping it would improve my performance. But it did not and so I was relegated to second level. I kept up with side-on and was now dropped for 3rd level. I gave it one last try and am now into the lowest level of my county—4th level. If I drop any further I would essentially be dropped from the team.

Do you reckon I should continue with side-on stance?

Yours sincerely,

A Wicket Keeper

Mr Faqih

Talking non-stop for days, about players with all sorts of names, cricket commentary can be a dangerous game. Brace yourself for some clangers.

- 'The bowler's Holding, the batsman's Willey.'
- 'He's usually a good puller—but he couldn't get it up that time.'
- 'Neil Harvey at leg slip, crouches, legs apart, waiting for a tickle.'
- 'It was an excellent performance in the field marred only when Harris dropped Crapp in the outfield.'
- 'Ray Illingworth has just relieved himself at the pavilion end.'
- 'You've just missed seeing Barry Richards hitting one of Basil D'Oliveira's balls clean out of the ground.'

But commentators aren't always caught out. When Pakistan's cricketers arrived in Australia in 1981, for example, some of the wiser heads saw the name 'Ijaz Faqih' on the team sheet and thought, 'What are we going to do?'

Their solution was to change his surname. The team sheet now read 'Ijaz F'.

'But how is it,' enquired one journo, 'that when I write f you see k?'

Douglas the disliked

Douglas Jardine didn't like Australians, and the feeling was very much mutual. In his home country, the name of the English cricket captain stands for cool-headed determination and implacable resolve. But on the other side of the world, you wouldn't be exaggerating if you said Jardine was the most hated cricketer to ever pollute an oval. His name is synonymous with snobbishness, cynicism and Pommie arrogance.

This dislike, of course, was at its height during the famous Bodyline series. When Jardine's side arrived in Australia in 1932, they brought with them a brand-new tactic. By crowding the pitch with fielders and bowling fast bouncers at the batsman's body, Jardine thought he might generate some catches—and with any luck, break some bones.

One day during the Sydney Test, he took a moment out from this assault and battery to brush away a fly that was buzzing nearby.

'Leave our flies alone, Jardine!' yelled a voice from the crowd. 'They're the only flamin' friends you've got here!'

Time for a change

Sometimes described as baseball on valium, cricket is not exactly a game for adrenaline junkies. If you're the sort of person who likes to hunt wild animals bare-handed, after a quiet morning's bungee-jumping, then it's unlikely to be your bag. There are many words to describe a long day spent standing in the outfield, or sitting in the dressing room waiting to bat, but 'electrifying' isn't one of them.

And cricketers need even more patience when they're captained by a guy like George Giffen. Australia's self-appointed 'engine room' of the 1890s, Giffen was an all-rounder who liked to bat for hours and, if at all possible, bowl for days. In one match, Giffen bowled every second over of an entire innings, and in another he bowled 87 overs out of a team total of 181.

During one such match, Giffen had been bowling for hours on end without a wicket when one of his underlings made a tactful suggestion. 'Maybe it's time for a change, captain?'

'Good idea,' replied the engine room. 'I'll come on from the other end.'

An embarrassment to the human race

The 2007 Cricket World Cup was held in the Caribbean and, in the end, it was a big success. But for a while there, this didn't look likely. There was a lot of negative media in the weeks leading up to the tournament, with some journalists attacking the way stadiums weren't quite finished, and others saying that the ticket prices were too high.

But one journo went too far. After a BBC reporter offered a few thoughts on the nation of Guyana, he woke up to a front-page article from its biggest newspaper, the *Kaieteur News*. Headlined 'Martin Gough's Insulting Journalism', the article declared that 'gutter journalism from a BBC Sport correspondent was the largest indication to date that British society has declined.'

'If Mr Gough's parents are alive, then one hopes they acknowledge that he is an embarrassment to the human race.

'The serpents and gorillas that live in Mr Gough's mind compelled him to descend to a level of pitiful, sickening and Hitleristic journalism about Guyana. Please don't come again, Mr Gough.'

He didn't.

The outrageous Cec

Cec Pepper had a colourful turn of phrase. 'The important thing in this game . . . is not how well you play but how much personality you project,' that Australian bowler once declared—and he liked to show his personality by appealing for a wicket whenever he could.

One fine day in Lancashire, 'the outrageous Cec' made a series of increasingly extravagant appeals, all of which were turned down by umpire George Long. Annoyed, he dropped a few F-bombs.

'Am I on report for my language?' Cec asked when the mood had finally passed.

'No', replied the Scottish umpire, 'Ah likes a chap as speaks his mind freely.'

Surprised and impressed, Pepper retrieved the ball and made ready to bowl it again. Running in, he managed to rap the batsman on the pad. Spinning around, he made his loudest appeal yet.

'Howzat?' Cec screamed. '*Howzaaaaaaaaaaaaaaaaat?*'

'Not out, you fat Australian bastard,' the umpire replied.

The six-inch urn

One of cricket's grand old traditions is warbling on endlessly about cricket's grand old traditions, so you'll be familiar with the story of the Ashes. When an Australian team first beat our colonial overlords, way back in 1882, a mock obituary appeared in an English newspaper mourning the 'death' of English cricket. The next year, when England came to play in Australia, a group of Melbourne ladies took the joke further. They presented the touring captain, Lord Darnley, with a six-inch urn containing the 'ashes' of English cricket—the burned remains of a bail or ball. Since that moment, these ashes have been the embodiment of cricket's greatest rivalry—a timeless, potent symbol of a timeless, potent feud.

Or at least, we *think* they have. A few decades ago, a former butler of Lord Darnley's sowed a seed of doubt. One day way back in the 1920s, he reported, a housemaid had come to him with a confession. She had knocked over 'that vase thing that stands on the mantelpiece in his Lordship's room' and discovered that it was full of ash.

But not to worry boss, the maid added. She'd given it 'a good clean out and polish before putting it back'.

Bouncers

Never the most popular of professions, bouncers got a particularly bad rap in late 1992 when a few of them combined to forcibly eject the NSW cricketer Greg Matthews from a nightclub and ended up putting him in a coma. The NSW team's manager, Neil Marks, was absolutely bombarded by interview requests for days, but was told to make himself unavailable for comment.

With one radio station, however, this proved pretty tough. They kept asking and asking and asking for an interview and, eventually, Marks acquiesced.

'I have with me Neil Marks, the manager of the NSW cricket team, whose high-profile member Greg Matthews is in a serious condition in hospital after allegedly being injured by a group of bouncers in a Perth nightclub two days ago,' said the host. 'This is not the first time that such a thing has happened in our city and later in the show we would like to know what you, our listeners, feel about this. Tell me, Mr Marks, what is your opinion of bouncers?'

'I believe that the rule allowing only one an over is stupid and should be changed immediately to at least two.'

JBW

Cricket is a game for philosophers; it teaches us to take the rough with the smooth. Every cricketer knows they'll be hurt by a bad umpiring decision one day—and then benefit from a bad one the next. The batsman who's been given out when they're not out knows that one day he'll be out but judged in. And the bowler who gets his man plumb LBW knows that there'll be some times when the umpire simply doesn't realise this—and other times when the ball would have sailed past the stumps but he for some reason raises his finger.

But even a philosopher would have lost his temper if he'd copped a decision like the one dealt to Tom Pugh. A capable 1960s batsman for Gloucestershire, Pugh was one day bracing himself to face David Larter, a frighteningly fast speed demon from Northamptonshire—a man who stood a muscular six foot, seven inches and began his run-up from the boundary rope.

And 'face' ended up being the operative word. Larter smashed a ball into Pugh's jaw, breaking it in a couple of places and forcing him to miss the next 18 games.

But that wasn't the bad part. He was also given out LBW.

Fettuccine and the Phantom

Cricketers can be a charitable bunch, and Richie Benaud is no exception. For one night every year, around the time of the Adelaide Test, he used to act as a 'guest chef' at a popular restaurant in that city, serving up fettuccine for all his fellow commentators in order to raise money for charity.

And every year, on the same night, Tony Greig would perform an equally important public service: he would try to get Billy Lawry drunk. This was a hard task as Bill's a teetotaller, but one night in 1987, Tony met with some unexpected success.

'Maybe it was the big-boobed waitress who enticed the "Phantom" into a glass of the demon bubbly, I don't know,' recalls Rod Marsh, 'but one glass led to four or five.'

Which, of course, led to many more. And Tony was with Bill every glass of the way, with the result that he vomited the famous Benaud fettuccine everywhere when he finally staggered back to his room.

The next morning, Tony's 12-year-old son left his pale, seedy dad sleeping, and saw an equally pale and seedy Bill Lawry on his way downstairs.

'Good morning, Mr Lawry. How are you today?'

'Mmmm . . . Mmmm . . . Not very well, thanks, Mark.'

'Oh. Did you eat some of Mr Benaud's fettuccine too?'

Tallon's triumph

We hear so much about the greatness of Don Bradman these days you could be forgiven for forgetting that there were other players. But actually, Australia had plenty of world-class cricketers back in the 1920s and 30s. Each had their own special skill sets and special stories of spectacular triumph. Take this tale told by Bill Tallon, a fast bowler who used to play for Queensland in the Sheffield Shield.

'We had to travel down south to Adelaide to play the Croweaters. We knocked over the first bastard and we had them one for one. We were bloody excited.

'Then out came Bradman. Everyone was full of expectancy. Everyone was doing their best, moving in with the bowler, really keen. Bradman was in a fair bit of bloody trouble. His timing was off, and the boys were rubbing their hands with glee.

'Eventually Alec Hurwood came on and Bradman hit the bloody thing so high in the air that every bastard tried to get under the catch, including the Queensland manager. We caught it! Two for 400!'

Harry's big innings

Life doesn't get too much more glorious than that moment when you score your first century. Though it's not as good as the moment when you score a double century, of course ... or a triple century ... or a quadru—but you get the idea. Holding your bat aloft to the cheering crowd, kissing your helmet as you lap up their screams: it's a moment that'll stay with you forever, provided you don't get too drunk.

Take pity, then, on poor Harry Makepeace—and not just because he had a naff surname. In 1907, the batsman notched up his very first century for Lancashire, his long, slow innings a master class in the virtue of patience and sound defensive technique. Once he reached 100 with a typically careful single, and acknowledged the roars of the crowd, Makepeace's captain declared the innings over, and sent the opposition in to bat.

Later, however, the scorers made a declaration of their own: they had added a leg-bye to Makepeace's score by mistake. For the next four years, until he finally did make a century, that batsman's best score was 99 not out.

John Major's baggy green

The former British PM John Major, son of a vaudeville performer, famously ran away from the circus to become an accountant. Then he took the whole debacle one step further and joined the Young Conservatives. Major's only saving grace, for anyone who ever has the misfortune to meet him at a dinner party, is his deep interest in cricket, a game he's described as a 'lifelong passion'.

In the course of that long life, Major was once given a baggy green cap by John Howard (another cricket-loving former PM). The Englishman says it's one of his most treasured possessions, but he's struggled to make other world leaders see the appeal of the game.

'I once tried to explain to an American president—and his eyes glazed over. He found it hard to comprehend a game could last over five days, but with no positive result. I tried it with Boris Yeltsin, too, over a large vodka. His eyes glazed over too, although—just perhaps—this was due to the vodka.'

The batsman's revenge

Batting is not '99% mental', as so many coaches like to say. A giant brain wouldn't be much use in front of the stumps without a bit of help from your arms and legs. But having said that, it's definitely important for a batsman to take it up to the bowler every now and then, and let them know he's ready to fight.

The English batsman Robin Smith provided a good example of this approach during the 1989 Ashes Test at Lord's. 'You can't bat,' he'd been told by Merv Hughes, after he played and missed a swerving delivery. 'You can't bat,' he was told again.

So next ball, Smith smashed Hughes to the boundary. 'Hey, Merv, we make a fine pair. I can't bat and you can't bowl.'

But far and away the best example of batsmanship belongs to a cricketer named Wilson Hartley, who played for Rochdale in the Central Lancashire League. Facing a fiery paceman named Peter Green one day, Hartley dodged and ducked some bouncers—and finally hooked one for a sensational six. It soared over the street and smashed the window of a nearby house. Which happened to belong to one Peter Green.

The model employee

No matter how high they might fly in the media, every journalist has a boss. Back when Richie Benaud was starting out in England, his big chief was one AP Wilkinson, the head of BBC Sport. Naturally, the young Richie would be on his best behaviour whenever Wilkinson was in the room. So one night, when they all shared a drink with their colleagues, he duly did his best to dazzle. And he might just have succeeded: Wilkinson actually offered to drive Richie and his wife home to their flat in Kensington, some 30 kilometres away.

'He was as bright as a button, chatting away on the way home,' Richie later wrote, 'and I was chatting with him.'

Until Richie fell asleep.

'From that moment on, Daphne did the chatting until we pulled up outside our London flat. Galvanised into action as the car stopped, I pulled out of my pocket the ten-pound note I had put there earlier for the taxi and said, "Thanks, driver, keep the change."'

Barclay's big fan

John Robert Troutbeck Barclay has a slightly odd middle name. But he never let this interfere with his cricket: the all-rounder amassed over 10,000 runs during his years as an opener at Sussex and took over 300 wickets with his off-spin. Sussex fans appreciate good cricket and Barclay was a popular fellow. His fans occasionally gathered by the boundary line, hoping to make eye contact with the great man or even exchange a few words.

On one occasion before a match against Middlesex, he found yet another one standing by. 'Mr Barclay,' she called out, 'have you won the toss?'

'Yes.'

'And are you going to bat?'

'Yes.'

'And are you opening the batting?'

'Yes.'

'In that case, I'll go to Hove to do my Sainsbury's shop before lunch.'

A new ball

Back in the 1930s, a new ball could only be taken after 200 runs had been scored. Seasickness pills, on the other hand, were taken all the time: the Australian cricket team's voyage to England was a long, slow and painful affair. And it often involved a stop in India, which was hardly good news for the belly.

During one such stop, the members of the Australian cricket team were rather ceremoniously presented to a very wealthy and influential maharajah, the ruler of somewhere near Bombay.

As the players stood in two neat lines awaiting the great moment of introduction, they were addressed by the team manager: 'I would like very much to introduce you to the Maharajah of Soandso. Not only is he the richest man in the world, he also has 199 wives.'

From the depths of the back row came: 'One more and he'd need a new ball!'

That wicket

Mike Brearley may not have been an especially great cricketer, but his man management was first rate. Put in charge of a hugely talented English Test team that had long been beset by division and squabbles, he did much to mend the cracks. Once described by a team mate as having 'a degree in people', Brearley is also a former president of the British Psychoanalytical Society, an internationally renowned expert on leadership and the author of *The Art of Captaincy*. Managing the different personalities and dynamics that make up a team, says Brearley, is largely about emotional intelligence. The good captain knows when to encourage, and when he needs to scold.

After one disastrous innings in 1979, on a very fast and green Perth wicket, this cricketing Freud decided that it was time to encourage. 'Don't worry, lads!' said the captain reassuringly. 'On that wicket, even Don Bradman wouldn't have got runs!'

'I should bloody well think he wouldn't,' replied a gloomy Bob Willis. 'He was born in 1908. He must be 71 by now!'

The love of a good woman

The love of a good woman, as most blokes know, can really bring out the best in a man. Faith and loyalty are more than just words: they are the very foundations of worldly success. The Indian cricketer BS Chandrasekhar met with plenty of success over the course of his career, but it was generally with a ball in his hand.

A renowned leg-spinner, Chandrasekhar averaged about four with the bat. The story goes that, while Chandrasekhar was playing in Chennai in 1979, his wife made a telephone call to the team's dressing room. 'Please fetch my husband,' she asked the attendant. 'There's some important information I need for the bank.'

'Sorry,' replied the attendant, 'he's just gone out to bat. Shall I get him to call back later?'

'No problem,' said Mrs Chandrasekhar, 'I'll wait on the line.'

The worst captain

In sports like footy and basketball, the captain just tosses the coin. Every now and then they might make a speech, pat a back or lift a trophy, but that's generally about as far as their duties go. In cricket, however, it's different: cricket captains have to think, think, think. Field placements and bowling changes. Team selections and batting orders. When to bat and who to bowl. What is the pitch doing? What about the weather? Should we declare? Will *they* declare? What will the papers say if we lose?

And on top of that, the captain also has to worry about what his team mates might say. Their expectations can be quite high.

The Australian Test medium pacer Neil Hawke, for example, once told Bill Lawry that he was 'the worst captain I ever played under. Twice you sent me in to bat in the middle of a hat-trick!'

A little man in glasses

These days, Tony Greig is mainly known as a commentator, but he was a pretty handy cricketer too. A batting average of 40, together with 141 wickets at 32.2, is nothing to sneer at.

Tony's heyday was the early 70s, so he was a natural choice for the Rest of the World side that was being assembled to play a game against Australia in 1971. He arrived at Adelaide airport with a team mate and was greeted by some local official.

'We were both itching to catch a glimpse of the real Australia and the little man in dark glasses and cardigan who approached us as we entered the transit lounge looked just the sort we had been hoping to avoid . . . We were just not in the mood . . . so we gave the little man our bags and slipped into the toilet to think of a way out.'

But there was no way out, it seemed: no escape from conversational gaol. Reluctantly bowing to the inevitable, Tony asked the man if he was connected with the Australian Board.

'Yes,' replied that elderly gent, still politely clutching Tony's bags.

'Played any cricket?'

'Yes.'

'Test cricket?'

'Yes.'

'Really? What's your name?'

'Don Bradman.'

Batting with Boycott

Cricket is a game of statistics: it's full of facts about who did what, where and when. Every Australian fan knows that the Don averaged 99.96, and Richie Benaud took 248 wickets. And every West Indian can remember that day at Antigua when Brian Lara scored 400 not out.

Stats and facts can never tell the whole story, however, for cricket is also a game of style. For the true cricket lover, an innings of, say, 20 can quite easily be better than an innings of 50: batting, for such connoisseurs, is not just about compiling runs, it's about compiling them in an elegant way. With nimble footwork and perfect balance. Economy of movement and purity of technique. These are the sorts of phrases you'll sometimes hear tossed around at Lord's—generally by some grumpy old buffer wearing two chins and a gravy-stained tie.

Geoffrey Boycott, the story goes, once got into an argument with David Gower about which of the two men had scored more centuries.

'I told you I've made more than you!' said Boycott, a notoriously dour batsman in his time.

'And thank God I've only seen three of them,' was the comment of a passerby.

AFL MOMENTS

The thing about football is, you've got to be prepared to go down for a mate.

Denis Pagan

Carrots and sticks

Modern coaches have to worry about what goes on in their players' heads, not just what goes on in the field. They have to think seriously about sports psychology and consult all sorts of experts in bright, white coats to figure out what's best for the team.

Back in the old days, things were easier: sports psychology basically boiled down to carrots and sticks. But coaches still had to know which were which. The story goes that, before one vitally important football game in 1975, Collingwood's coach, Murray Weideman, thought that it might be a good time to dangle a carrot.

'Win this one,' he told his boys, 'and the whole lot of you are on a trip to Fiji!'

Bullseye! Fingers twitched and sinews stiffened. As one, the players straightened their shoulders and got the battle gleam back in their eyes. You could almost hear their muscles flex, their fighting spirit give a bellow and roar.

Much encouraged, Weideman went on: 'And what's more, we'll invite your wives along as well!'

Needless to say, they lost.

God help St Kilda

In late September 2009, a massive red dust storm swept across eastern Australia. Over 1000 kilometres long and some 500 kilometres wide, the freak incident was probably the result of an intense north low-pressure area that picked up a lot of dust from the continent's interior.

That's one explanation, anyway. Another theory is that someone opened the door to St Kilda's trophy cabinet. The winner of one AFL premiership and some *twenty-six* wooden spoons, the mighty St Kilda Football Club has a long and grim history of failure. Whatever the circumstances, and whoever the opponent, its players have always found a new way to fail.

But enough negativity, let's think positively. Or, at least, let's quote a player who tried to do that. 'Oh well, at least there were no injuries,' said the St Kilda stalwart in 1951, after the club had lost a game by 130 points.

'How could there be?' replied his somewhat less positive coach. 'None of you buggers got close enough to the opposition to get knocked over!'

John Bourke, ice man

One of the frustrations of life in AFL is that good players tend to get tagged. It's the tagger's job to make sure that their opponent doesn't get the ball. Instead of kicking, marking and handballing, a tagger's key skills are niggling, pinching and annoying. They will follow a star wherever he goes, and say all sorts of nasty things about his mum. Some stars cope quite well with this, and never once lose their composure. With the cold-blooded calm of a champion, these sorts of players simply lift their work rate, and play a bit harder or smarter.

Other players cope less well. Collingwood full-back John Bourke, for example, probably did lose his cool a little bit back in 1985, when he was tagged during a game against the Swans. Close observers could tell he wasn't handling it well by the way he kicked the tagger in the groin. And then hit an official from his own team. And then kicked and pushed the umpire. And then ran into the stands to attack a fan.

Getting through to Crazy Horse

There are all sorts of ways that a coach can get through to his players. Some respond well to a rocket, others like the sound of sweet reason. Some players need to be told that they're special, others that they're part of a team. Some players like lots of detail, while others can't even spell the word. In short, sportspeople can be babies and adults, and pretty much every age in between.

Enter the difficult teenager. Some players just can't be gotten through to, no matter what a coach might try. Ron Barassi had this problem when he was coaching North Melbourne with a player called Gary 'Crazy Horse' Cowton. One time, it's said, Barrassi was trying and failing to make a point and very suddenly reached the end of his tether.

'Son, what is it with you?' he shouted. 'Is it ignorance or apathy?'

Crazy Horse considered this for a moment. 'Barassi,' he eventually replied, 'I don't know and I don't care.'

A need for speed

'The pain of discipline is far less than the pain of regret,' as some athlete once said. Obviously, they were lying. What could possibly be more painful, for example, than the sort of training required to win an AFL premiership? Day after day, from dawn until dusk, these super-fit super-freaks sweat their way through the weights room, the grounds and the gym. They must meet with physiotherapists, nutritionists and conditioning specialists. To me, it sounds like hell.

I'd have much rather played footy in the 1960s, when training involved one or two laps around the oval, followed by three beers and a dozen fags. You could run like an asthmatic hamster and still play a pretty good game.

One time, it's said, a great but glacially slow champion of that era, Kevin 'Cowboy' Neale, noticed that his coach had forgotten to bring a stopwatch to training.

'How are you going to time our laps, boss?'

'In your case, with a sundial.'

The law of the jungle

'Rugby football,' PG Wodehouse once remarked, 'is a game I can't claim absolutely to understand in all its niceties. I can follow the broad, general principles, of course. I mean to say, the main scheme is to work the ball down the field somehow and deposit it over the line at the other end. In order to squelch this program, each side is allowed to put in a certain amount of assault and battery and do things to its fellow man, which, if done elsewhere, would result in 14 days without the option, coupled with some strong remarks from the Bench.'

Australian Rules Football, Wodehouse would be glad to know, is a little bit more civilised. The rules may allow players to assault and batter one another, but they draw a clear, thick line at murder. During one match in the 1940s, Richmond hard man Jack Dyer became worried that he'd crossed that line after a sickening collision with a Melbourne ruckman. The player fell to the ground like a sack of potatoes, and was stretchered off, motionless, with a white sheet over his head.

'My God!' Dyer exclaimed to Richmond's vice-president at half-time. 'He's dead! I can't play in the second half. I've murdered that poor bastard.'

But the vice-president happened to be a criminal lawyer—and a pretty good amateur psychologist. 'Go out there and play the game of your life in the second half,' he told Jack. 'Win it for us and I'll get you off on a manslaughter charge.'

The elephant in the room

Harry Beitzel was a pioneer in AFL broadcasting, and the man most responsible for the International Rules games between Australia and Ireland. But his career also included a conviction for lottery fraud.

Shortly after his release from 18 months' jail, Beitzel made an appearance on *The Footy Show*. For several tactful minutes, the panellists carefully avoided the elephant in the room. They asked questions about anything and everything, except Beitzel's time in jail.

After several minutes, he was politely thanked for coming on the show and the host began to throw to a commercial. Cue a loud interjection from the comedian Trevor Marmalade: 'Hey Harry, you dropped your car keys!'

Reaching beneath the desk, Marmalade then retrieved a coat hanger, bent all out of shape.

The heavenly Hudson

The biggest star known to Hawthorn fans is Peter Hudson. A record-breaking full-forward in both the Tasmanian League and the AFL, Huddo kicked 727 goals in the brown and gold stripes during the 1960s and 70s, at the extraordinary average of 5.59 a game. A Member of the Order of Australia, he was inducted into the Australian Football Hall of Fame in 1996 and elevated to official Legend status three years later.

Of course, he'd already been an unofficial legend for quite a while. In the weeks leading up to the 1970 grand final, a church billboard in the Melbourne suburb of Hawthorn asked the following question of passersby: 'What would you do if God came to Hawthorn today?'

The answer, according to one graffiti artist, was: 'Move Peter Hudson to centre half-forward.'

'When I tell the story outside Hawthorn,' said Melbourne academic Peter Turner, 'they ask, "Who's Peter Hudson?" When I tell the story in Hawthorn, they ask, "Who's God?"'

That bloody triangle

Australian football requires athleticism, skill and speed. It does not, however, require brains.

Two former players, Len Thompson and Max Richardson, may have helped to reinforce this truth when they went on an end-of-the-season trip in 1980. Former team mates at Collingwood who had recently been reunited at Fitzroy, they decided to get together for some boozy snooker, a game neither man had played before. They took to it like ducks to slaughter—'non-existent' is one way to describe their skills, though a better word might be 'unforgivable'. Finally, after about 60 minutes had passed, and not a single ball had been potted, Max Richardson made a bold suggestion.

'Look, we've been here an hour or more and haven't sunk a ball. We're starting to make bloody dings of ourselves. What do you think about a bit of cheating?'

'I'll be in a bit of cheating any time,' replied Thompson. 'What do you have in mind?'

'Well, for a start, why don't we take that bloody triangle off the table?'

A hero returns

The heart and soul of the Melbourne Football Club is called Ronald Dale Barassi. One of the most celebrated players in AFL history and an official Legend in the league's Hall of Fame, Barassi led Melbourne to an extraordinary six premierships and remains its most famous son.

But at some stage, all sons leave home. The Melbourne champion broke many hearts in 1964 when he accepted a lucrative offer to move to Carlton, amid an unprecedented media storm. 'Inevitably, with many decisions in life there will be a downside,' was his comment at the time. 'It is regrettable but you have to get on with things.'

And then, a few years later, he went and moved again. In 1974, Barassi accepted an offer to coach North Melbourne. He later took the club to its first ever premiership.

But did he take it into his heart? Maybe not. In 1980, Melbourne supporters rejoiced as one when big Ron came back to the fold. Having accepted an offer to coach the club of his youth, Barassi attended the club's annual general meeting to a chorus of cheers and tears.

'Ladies and gentlemen,' he declared, after taking the stage, 'it's great to be back at North Melbourne once again . . .'

Shitzroy

As children, we're often told that winning or losing is unimportant; what matters is how you play the game. Fitzroy played the game very badly. Now no longer with us—the club merged with the Brisbane Lions in 1996—Fitzroy's 99-year history combined long periods of mediocrity with several years of being completely shit. Constantly destitute and with diabolical training facilities, supporting Fitzroy would have been a bit like supporting the *Titanic* had that ship been built with less money and style.

But so what? said the fans ('it's not whether you win or lose, etc'). One such diehard was the TV star Bert Newton. One time, after going to watch yet another comprehensive thrashing, it's said Bert took a friend along for a drink with a few other Fitzroy supporters.

'Blimey, Bert, look at all the hilarity,' commented the friend. Despite the loss, he noticed, everybody's spirits were high. 'What happens when Fitzroy actually wins?'

'I don't know,' replied Bert. 'I have to ask one of the older members.'

One boy's toys

A coach can talk to his heart's content, and say some brilliant and insightful things. But if his players aren't listening, it won't matter a jot. For that reason, it's important for coaches to mix things up a bit—to keep delivering the same old message in fun, new and different ways. A four-time premiership coach of the AFL club Melbourne took just this tack in the 1930s. Frank 'Checker' Hughes gathered his boys together after a sorry first half in which they'd played without energy or brains.

'Once upon a time, when I was a very young boy,' Checker began, as mild as a kitten, 'my mother bought me eighteen red and blue wooden soldiers. I learned to love and know each and every one of them. I used to play with them for hours on end.

'I really loved them,' he went on softly, 'even though all they did was to stand in the same spot looking woodenly ahead without doing anything.

'Finally, the sad day came when I lost them. I searched for them everywhere without ever seeing them again. Until today, *when I've got the whole bloody pack of you back again*!'

The Mayblooms

Brown and gold are the colours of the Hawthorn Football Club. They are also the colours of poo and urine. In the club's early decade, this was not wholly inappropriate. Originally nicknamed the Mayblooms, Hawthorn were the whipping boys of the competition for the first 17 years of their existence, never winning more than seven games in a season. And after that, they were even worse. Between 1944 and 1953, the club's best end-of-year result was second last. If Hawthorn players happened to be known as good losers, this was only because they got lots of practice.

Unsurprisingly, this lack of success took its toll on crowd numbers. Hawthorn's support base was confined to people who lived near the ground, and people who hated life. Once, it's said, during yet another bad patch in 1980, a fan phoned the club's headquarters to ask what time the match started the following Saturday.

'What time can you get here?' Hawthorn's president anxiously replied.

The constipated cricketer

Constipation can be pretty funny. Who hasn't heard the one about the constipated accountant (he couldn't budget) or the constipated mathematician (he worked it out with a pencil). And if you can't smile at the constipated *Wheel of Fortune* player who wanted to buy a bowel, then you probably can't smile at all. These are good, solid gags, and not to be pooh-poohed.

But when you've actually got constipation yourself, you really don't give a crap. You just want to get to the bottom of the problem and solve it, whatever it takes. When the Victorian cricketer and AFL footy coach Ray 'Slug' Jordan was so afflicted, for example, he certainly didn't laugh; he took a trip to the doctor.

As Slug had been a colonic underachiever for days, the doc said some suppositories were required. Now Slug had never heard of suppositories, but he figured he'd give them a go. A few days later, however, he was right back at the doctor's, reporting no movement at the station.

'Did you take the suppositories?'

'Sure. I took one with a glass of water each day, but for all the good they did, I might as well have stuck them up my bum!'

Danny's moment

AFL history is packed with inspirational speeches, from John Kennedy's *'Do something!'* to Teddy Whitten's 'Stick it up 'em!' Nothing beats the sound of a crazy-eyed coach with a visibly throbbing jugular, exhorting his boys to give their all for the cause.

An address from Richmond reserves coach Danny Guinane may not quite belong in this glittering pantheon, but it probably deserves to be remembered anyway. It came at half-time during a game in the early 1940s, in which Richmond were being comprehensively thrashed.

The senior coach, Jack Dyer, was so disgusted with the team's efforts that he stormed out of the dressing room and gave his junior the floor. 'I've had teams which were 12 goals down at half-time. Maybe even 13 goals down, but never 16 goals down, not at half-time. Danny, you're on your own.'

This was Danny's moment, and he didn't disappoint. 'Boys,' he began, 'I don't have to tell you how badly you played in the first half. You know. But forget that now and listen to what I want you to do in the second half. What I want you to do is to go out on the ground and pick up your man. Stand about a foot in front of him and look him in the eye. Then—this is the important part—turn your back on him, drop your shorts, bend over and let him finish the job.'

HORSE
RACING
MOMENTS

Horse racing is animated roulette.

Roger Kahn

The tale of Trodmore

A sure thing is pretty hard to find in gambling, as quite a few of my bank statements show. But it's generally a pretty safe bet that journalists will be lazy.

A Mr G Martin of Cornwall took just such a bet in 1898, when he wrote to the editors of *The Sportsman* and asked them to cover an upcoming race. He supplied the names and local odds of the horses that were due to run in the Trodmore Hunt Steeplechase, and promised to wire in the results after the race.

The Sportsman duly advertised the date of the race and many readers duly placed their bets. And when Mr Martin advised that the favourite, a stallion named Reaper, had won, many bookies duly paid out.

Several weeks passed before someone realised that Reaper hadn't, in fact, won. In large part, this was because he didn't exist. There was no such thing as the Trodmore Hunt Steeplechase, or indeed a place called Trodmore.

We'll never ever know who 'Mr Martin' was, but we can probably guess which horse he backed.

The old switcheroo

Many people love a good horse race—including, I'm sad to say, crims. Plenty of great criminal minds have turned their attention to the track over the years, often with very lucrative results. But you couldn't call the owners of a racehorse called Fine Cotton great criminal minds. It's debatable whether they had minds at all.

Familiar to many in racing, the story of Fine Cotton began in 1984. A syndicate bought a promising racehorse of that name, who turned out to be rather slow. After a few big losses were followed by a few even bigger losses, the syndicate decided to pull the old switcheroo: get a horse that can actually run, tell people it's Fine Cotton, then watch it storm home at long odds.

Not a bad idea. *Provided the horse actually looked like Fine Cotton.* The one they chose didn't. Not even after they changed the colour of his coat with hair dye and house paint.

An incredible run

Every now and then in sport, a champion is born. In soccer, he might arrive with an impossible goal; in rugby, with a freakish try. And what punter doesn't know the thrill of seeing an unknown stallion suddenly burst out of the pack and gallop home to glory and fame?

Alf Gard once had this thrill at Victoria Park, an Adelaide racecourse that sits next to a highway. The veteran race caller, who fell in love with racing at age eight when his father took him to see Phar Lap, thought that here at last was a worthy successor to the great Melbourne Cup winner.

'It's an incredible run!' Gard gasped on air, when a jockey wearing red silks and a black cap made an extraordinarily quick break from the pack. 'I have never seen anything like it! He's absolutely storming past the field, on the outside—absolutely mowing them down!'

His excitement dampened a few seconds later. 'That's not a horse and jockey, you twit,' said Gard's fellow caller. 'It's a bloke in a red jumper and black helmet on a motorbike on the road outside.'

Nude in Doncaster

There have been streakers in sport since at least 1804, when a student named George Crump went tackle-out to a football game. He later went on to become a US Congressman. But streaking's pinnacle came almost two centuries later: 1974 was a bonanza year for boobs lovers, and a great chance to giggle at willies. There was a streaker at the Academy Awards, a streaker in a sitcom and a song named 'The Streak' in the charts. Literally thousands of streaks took place across the world, while more buttoned-up types could wear a watch with a naked Richard Nixon, or pink underwear labelled 'too shy to streak'.

But not everyone was able to get in on the act. Once, at the 1974 Doncaster Handicap in Sydney, a naked man and woman jumped the fence and made their jiggly way towards the horse enclosure, where TV cameras were to be found. It was locked.

'Open it up!' they cried. 'We have to get in, the horses are coming.'

'No! You can't come in here.'

'Why?'

'Because you haven't got a ticket!'

Young Whack

Sportspeople have cheated ever since sport was invented, but it's only recently that they've begun to cheat well. Not knowing all that much about, well, anything, some ancient Olympians would drink a performance-enhancing elixir made out of mushrooms—or, if that failed, they'd tuck into bull testicles. Lizard's flesh, eaten in a certain way, was also thought to have magical properties, while Roman charioteers fed their horses wine. Even at the 1904 Olympics, some 2000 years later, a marathon runner named Thomas Hicks almost died after mixing brandy and strychnine in an effort to put pep in his step.

Nowadays, however, cheats seem to know what they're doing, which made the results of a 2001 drug test not a little surprising. The Dublin Turf Club found that a racehorse named Young Whack had a stimulant in his blood, but one that wasn't very stimulating: nicotine. The racehorse had presumably come across a tobacco pouch some time in his travels and decided that it was time for a snack.

Young Whack had to be disqualified from the race but his owner took the blow with good grace. 'He'll be some horse when we get him off the fags!'

Penny-pinching with Piggott

Lester Piggott would be the first to tell you he's fond of money. Once jailed for tax evasion, the champion British jockey 'relishes every crisp fiver like some rare jewel', according to fellow rider, Bill Rickaby. 'Money is his stuff of life and he ekes it out as sparingly as a man faced with 50 years of unpensionable retirement.'

An Australian racing identity once took Piggott around the country for a month—and reports that he didn't pay for anything at all. Even at a milk bar, John Scott recalled, Piggott simply 'picked up an ice-cream and walked out. "You've got to pay for that," I told him. He didn't. I did.'

On another occasion, legend has it, the partially deaf Piggott was approached by a punter who was down on his luck. He asked Piggott to spot him a tenner.

'Sorry, you've got me on my deaf side. Talk to me in the other ear.'

'Hey Lester, can you lend me £20?'

'Go back to the other side. I liked it better when you asked for £10.'

Hauled before the committee

Horse racing, say some people, can be quite corrupt. These are the people who know something about it. A tale from a former Turf Club steward, Jim Marsh, helps to illustrate the point—though naturally, its cast must stay nameless. A well-known jockey, reports Marsh, was once suspected of taking a very good horse and deliberately making it run a bad race. Had someone fixed the race? Had they slipped him a bag of cash?

Good questions, requiring good answers. The jockey was hauled before a racing club committee—several stern, grey men in stern, grey suits—and shocked all of them by owning up.

'Did you pull this horse on your own initiative or on instructions?' the astonished chairman asked him.

'On instruction from the owners, sir.'

'Good heavens! Have you done this sort of thing for other owners?'

'I have, sir.'

'Who were these owners?'

The jockey pointed at some of the other committee members. 'Him, him and him, to name just three.'

Birth of a word

The secret of success is a secret—but I'm happy to let you in on it.

OK, here goes: success has nothing to do with 'positive thinking' or 'never stopping learning' or 'being persistent and working hard'. It's just a question of lowering expectations. If other people expect nothing, all you have to do is *something*—and, wham, you're a raging success.

The other side of this coin is failure. It only comes when you've promised the world. The sport of horse racing, for example, has always been chock-full of the slow, old and crap. Horses that can barely run and horses that can barely walk. Horses that keep falling over and horses that stop for a rest mid-race. But by and large, when they achieve nothing, we remember nothing. We forget their failure because we never expected success.

One bad racehorse, however, is still remembered by one and all—and that's because people were told he'd be good. He arrived on the Australian racing scene in a blaze of glory in 1921, owners, journos and punters all predicting great things. But while the horse had all the speed needed to hit the lead, he surrendered it every time. He ran 37 races and lost 37 races.

His name, we should probably add, was Drongo.

RUGBY
MOMENTS

Rugby is played by men with odd-shaped balls.

Bumper sticker

A Scotsman never forgets

The Scots have a certain reputation for stinginess. Years and years of irresponsible jokes (like this one: How do you disperse an angry mob in Scotland? Tell them you're taking up a collection) have given them a certain image.

But some real Scotsmen have also helped. The Scottish Rugby Union international Ian Robertson, for example, swears that once before a match against England, he took some journalists to a small restaurant in Edinburgh that he hadn't been to in over 30 years.

'How marvellous to see you again, Mr Robertson,' said the unsmiling maître d. 'I imagine you have come to pay the one shilling sixpence [approximately 12 cents in today's money] you owe us for the single malt whisky you drank when you were last here and forgot to pay for?'

Not his fault

Once upon a time, all a rugby player needed to know was where the try line was, and whether his team mates were the ones in the red tops. Admittedly, a lot of them still found this challenging, but with the right training and some appropriate memory cues, things were generally sorted out in the end.

More recently, however, the game has become complicated, a baffling concoction of attacking formations and defensive patterns. A team training session is all about tactics and drills and phases and strategies, which can be painful for both body and mind.

It's even more painful when you're the new boy. In 1973, John Lambie was selected in a NSW team to play Tonga. The coach, Dave Brockhoff, was running drills on a defensive pattern Lambie was unfamiliar with, and the new boy immediately found himself 40 metres out of position.

'When I tell you to do something, you bloody well do it!' yelled a furious Brockhoff, humiliating his vulnerable young charge. But then his voice changed, his expression softened and the player began to feel better.

'Lambie, it's not your fault. It's the selectors' fault. You shouldn't be here.'

Straight talk with Slab

Some rugby coaches wear kid gloves—but Slab Allan preferred a knuckle-duster. An old school First World War veteran whose body still held shrapnel from the Somme, Slab was the quintessential straight-talker— nuggety, hard and tough.

'Sometimes I will hurt you and you may not like it,' he told his boys after taking charge of Gordon Rugby Club. 'Well, that's your problem because I don't give a bucket of horseshit what you think. If anyone present can't take being criticised, I suggest that he piss off out of here right now.'

Merv Nagle could take being criticised, as he proved after one match in which he'd tried to daintily dribble a ball through the mud.

'You looked like a bloody ballet dancer!' thundered Slab. 'When the ball is in the mud, kick the bloody thing as far as you can.'

Then the coach stormed over to a ball on the floor of the dressing room, and proceeded to demonstrate. The ball smashed into a mirror, sending glass all over a player's face.

'Don't be concerned about me, Slab, I'm quite OK,' said the player, shards sticking out of his forehead, blood running over his face.

'I'm not worried about you, you silly bugger. Look what's happened to the mirror!'

No pain, no gain

'Cycling is so hard, the suffering is so intense, that it's absolutely cleansing,' seven-time Tour de France winner Lance Armstrong once observed. 'The pain is so deep and strong that a curtain descends over your brain . . . Once, someone asked me what pleasure I took in riding for so long. "*Pleasure?*" I said. "I don't understand the question. I didn't do it for the pleasure; I did it for the pain."'

Lance Armstrong, clearly, is nuts. Fortunately, not all sports list this as a requirement. While rugby union, for example, involves getting tackled quite a bit, it's basically a sport for people who prefer to avoid intense suffering—for people who, on the whole, prefer not to diet, let alone jog, when they could just drive a car.

'Don't worry, the game will fly by,' a veteran player once called out to a young debutant called Paul Ackford. 'You'll find the first half seems like three minutes and the second half four minutes.'

'You're a damn liar!' gasped Ackford a few minutes later. 'I've been out here for four-and-a-half hours and the game's still not over.'

Swallow your medicine

The comedian Peter Cook once recalled the first time he played rugby at school. 'I fell on a loose ball and, through ignorance and fear, held on despite a fierce pummelling. After that it took me months to convince my team mates I was a coward.'

Cook might as well have tried convincing his team mates he was sensible. Academics at the Centre for International Public Health Policy have recently called for rugby to be banned in schools. Their survey found that for every 1000 hours a school player is on the pitch, they tend to receive 10.8 injuries. 'If youngsters were coming back from school trips with these rates of injuries it would be enough to trigger a major inquiry,' they accurately state.

But what the good professors may not realise is that— rugby players being, well, rugby players—they're just as likely to come to harm off the pitch. A good example is supplied by turn-of-the-century league player Alf 'Bullock' Dobbs, who finished a game against Newcastle in 1908 with a sprained ankle and two black eyes.

A little while later, his team mates considerately placed a jug of water with four leeches in it beside his bed, so he could apply the leeches to his eyes when he eventually woke up.

When they came back, the jug was empty and the leeches were gone. Big Bullock had dutifully swallowed his medicine.

The Anzac spirit

On 25 April 1915, soldiers from the Australian and New Zealand Army Corps landed on a narrow, rocky beach in Turkey, and proceeded to build a legend. Over 8000 Anzac soldiers died in that ill-fated campaign, but their courage lives on to this day. Gallipoli gave Australians a sense of who they were as a people; it was the moment that a few recently federated colonies became a nation instead.

Anzac Day, therefore, can get very evocative. Rosemary is worn, minute-long silences are observed and solitary bugles play a sombre tune. And if you were anywhere near Coogee Oval on 25 April 1970, you would have heard the coach of Sydney University's rugby team urging his boys to show some 'Anzac spirit'.

'This is Anzac Day, men,' bellowed the legendary motivator, David Brockhoff, after discreetly loosening the hinges on the dressing room door. 'We are playing Randwick, the outright enemies. This is Turkey for us. If it was good enough for the boys at Gallipoli, it's good enough for us, and today, fellas, *we do battle*!'

With that he strode to the door and kicked it down. 'Follow me out! Over the top!'

Come half-time, they were down 17–3.

Caring for Tommy

The medical services on hand in Australian sport these days really are state of the art. In the AFL, for example, there are always several doctors on hand. Trainers and physiotherapists are given strict guidelines about what to do in cases of concussion, and precautionary measures include always putting an injured player in a neck brace, and placing the stretcher on a golf cart instead of carrying it to ensure a smooth ride to the doc.

In England, things sometimes go a little less smoothly. A Rugby Union player named Tommy Martin, for example, once sustained a bad ankle injury and had to be stretchered off the ground. Unfortunately for Tommy, the ground's one and only stretcher was already being used to transport another player to an ambulance.

After waiting five minutes for a stretcher, the crowd was growing impatient, so two desperate club officials grabbed an old office chair from the clubhouse and rushed it out onto the pitch. They lifted Martin into the chair and began to carry him off, straining under his considerable weight.

Just as they got him off the grass and onto the concrete that led to the dressing rooms, a huge crack was heard around the ground. The chair broke, leaving the officials holding the armrests. Martin lay crumpled on the ground, having landed ankle first.

Clamp down on that, son

Rugby, Oscar Wilde once remarked, is 'a good technique for keeping 30 bullies far from the centre of the city'. Unfortunately for the people who play it, this involves putting 29 other bullies very close to them. Gruesome rugby injuries over the years have included snapped ankles, broken necks and bruised eyeballs, as well as torn scrotums and bitten-off tongues. The Dalai Lama believes that 'all suffering is caused by ignorance', but he's clearly never been in a scrum.

Even *watching* this game can be dangerous. In his debut game for the Sydney club Northern Suburbs, a second rower named Justin Nowlan got a belt on the jaw and later suggested that it might be broken.

'Clamp down on that, son,' said a helpful club patron, sticking a finger into his mouth. 'We'll soon see if it's broken.'

Nowlan dutifully clamped.

'Son, your jaw's not broken but I might need a tetanus needle before the next game.'

Feet on the ground

A challenge for modern-day sports stars is keeping their ego in check. There's just so much adulation to cope with; so many cheers from the fans. One can only hope that they keep in touch with old mates, and have a family that keeps their feet on the ground.

Former Wallaby forward John Lambie was an Australian rugby great during the 70s—and, as such, got a great deal of love. Even after his playing career ended, the moustachioed player remained in much demand, as he related in his book, *Well I'll Be Ruggered*.

One time, the champ recalled, he was invited to speak at the all-female View Club in Gunnedah, a NSW country town. 'I arrived for the dinner and was met by the president who ushered me through a room of women. It was quite obvious that I was the centre of their attention.'

'The president bought me a beer and then took a pen and paper to take down some details to introduce me. She firstly asked me to spell my name. Having done that, she looked at me in embarrassment and exclaimed, "John Lambie? We thought we were getting John Landy."'

A man of the people

Politics and sport aren't always the safest mix. The former Aussie prime minister Gough Whitlam found this out the hard way in 1975, when he was invited to toss the coin at the rugby league grand final by the president of the Queensland Rugby League, Ron McAuliffe. Now the PM was a Grecian scholar and lover of the arts, a man for whom sport was about as interesting as socks. But there was an election coming up, so why not press some flesh?

But as he strode out on to Lang Park with McAuliffe in tow, Whitlam didn't get quite the reception he'd hoped for. 'The mob went berserk,' recalled writer Barry Cohen. 'They hissed, booed, threw meat pies, beer cans and anything they could lay their hands on to show their affection for Gough and the Labor Party. When they finally quietened down, Gough kicked off.'

And then he (metaphorically) kicked McAuliffe. As they walked off, the PM turned to his companion and said: 'Ron, if I knew you were this unpopular, I would never have come to the match.'

Convalescing with Mr Clues

Staring death in the face is an unnerving experience that people approach in different ways: philosophers get philosophical and the spiritual begin to pray. Arthur Clues watched rugby.

When Clues was hospitalised after a heart attack, the former Western Suburbs and Australian Rugby League player spent some of his convalescence watching the English Cup final. Doctors and nurses warned him to sit quietly in bed for the sake of his ticker, but Arthur ignored them, largely because he was so busy pacing around the hospital ward and yelling excitedly at the screen.

Then, suddenly, tragedy struck. The patient in the next bed passed away. Upset, Clues sought out the doctor.

'Mr Clues, will you please get back into bed? I've told you before to stay in bed and remain calm.'

'But, doc,' he protested, distraught, 'the poor bugger was interested in the cup final and he's died without ever knowing the final score.'

'Mr Clues, if you continue to carry on as you are, you'll be able to tell him the result personally.'

Time for a rousing speech

There is more to sport than just winning. Sadly, there is losing as well. For every team that storms home to victory, there has to be a bunch of chumps trudging back to the change rooms, trying to avoid eye contact with the crowd.

At a rugby union international in 1966, the Australian team was getting ready to trudge. Despite recent big wins against the All Blacks and the Springboks—and the fact that their opponents were England—the highly rated Aussies went into the half-time break down 31–0. What the hell was going on?

It was clearly time for a rousing speech—ideally something about patriotism and why it justifies all kinds of violence. But the coach decided to try to reason with his players instead.

'Listen fellows,' said John Thornett, a softly spoken university graduate. 'This just isn't us.'

'All right,' piped up a voice from the back. 'If it isn't us, what do you say we piss off?'

A fear of nudity

Some athletes are motivated by fear of failure; others have to overcome a fear of success. Edward Fry had a fear of nudity, and it was crucial to his success. Fry was an outstanding rugby centre who represented NSW against Queensland in 1892. But he was so overcome with pride when he put on the light blue jersey that he forgot underpants can be useful as well.

Predictably enough, someone tried to tackle him during the match, and ended up with a handful of shorts. Stark naked from willy to shin, and in full view of his fiancé and mum, Fry made a break for where the crowd seemed thinnest—which just happened to be beside the NSW try line.

He threw himself at the line and stayed there until another pair of shorts was found. The try is still recognised as one of the finest individual efforts of the period.

The last resort

Patriotism may be the last resort of the scoundrel, but it's the first port of call for a national coach. When Clive Rowlands took control of the Welsh rugby union team in 1968, he never hesitated to beat the drum. Despite the fact that they lived in a small, wet country, mostly filled with coal mines and sheep, players under Rowland took pride in their jumper, and did whatever it took to win.

In large part, this was down to his inspirational pre-match speeches—rousing and emotion-filled calls to arms. But sometimes they were a bit *too* inspirational, as was the case before a match against the All Blacks.

'What are you going to do?' Rowlands screamed, at the end of his blood-and-thunder address to the troops.

'*Win!*' they screamed back.

'What are we going to do?' he repeated, more loudly.

'Win, win . . . *win!*'

And it seemed that a player named Geoff Wheel couldn't wait to start. Shouting 'Kill, *kill*!' he suddenly leaped up and raced towards the pitch in a patriotic frenzy. Unfortunately a door was in the way, and he butted a hole clean through it.

BOXING
MOMENTS

Boxing is like a ballet, except there's no music, no choreography and the dancers hit each other.

Jack Handy

Trouble in bowel country

There are many different ways to lose a boxing match—and some boxers experience them all. You can be overly defensive or overly aggressive, go for too many clinches or forget to duck. Some boxers just feint and jab and never do any real damage, while other boxers don't jab enough, being too preoccupied with the knockout punch.

A less common way to lose involves old-fashioned diarrhoea. This was the sad fate that befell Andrew 'Runny Bum' Lewis in his national title fight against 'Deadly' Denny Dalton. The junior middleweight had been forced to make a few quick toilet stops before the 12-round bout, after he was given a homemade milkshake by a member of his camp—'it just caused my belly to go off'—but he seemed to have recovered by the time he got into the ring.

Midway through the seventh round, Lewis was well on top—only to suddenly feel trouble below the belt. He abruptly quit and left the ring. 'It was as bad as that. If I had stayed longer in the ring I would have messed my skin.' Life can be a bit crap sometimes.

A bit of straight talk

Sports journalists who cover boxing know to pick their words with care. They are dealing, after all, with the professionally violent: men who are trained to punch first and think later—then punch, punch, punch again.

Cas Adams was an exception to this rule. His journalism was frank, forthright and fearless. He called it as he saw it, and he saw 'Two Ton' Tony Galento as a bum. A 'no-holds barred' heavyweight who once fought a 250 kilogram bear, Galento certainly would have *had* a bum. While in training, he would eat six chickens for every meal, and wash them down with a bowl of spaghetti.

Anyway, Adams—being frank, forthright, etc—tried to interview Galento at one of his training sessions not too long after the 'bum' comment.

'You ain't welcome here,' the big boxer growled. 'I don't like them things you've been saying about me.'

'I wrote that you were a bum,' said Adams fearlessly, 'and I reiterate it!'

'Well, that's different. I accept your apology.'

The Greatest

Muhammad Ali was the greatest, as he often liked to tell us himself. Able to float like a butterfly and sting like a bee, feint like a mongoose and hit passing fleas, Ali was a 20th-century icon. He remains the only man in history to win the World Heavyweight Championship three times.

Of course, this means that he was the only man in history to *lose* the World Heavyweight Championship three times. *Sports Illustrated* declared Ali Sportsman of the Century in large part because he was sport's *personality* of the century. An articulate social activist who refused to fight in the Vietnam War, that boxer complemented his big mouth with a big heart. He always gave good interview, and he gave a lot to charity as well.

One time, the champ was told that a Jewish old person's home in New York was to be torn down. Ever so quietly, Ali handed over enough money to build a new home, and when it was done, paid a discreet visit.

'Do you know who this is?' said Ali's trainer, introducing him to one of the residents.

'Yeah, it's the champ.'

'That's right.'

'I know him. He's the greatest. He's Joe Louis.'

Eye of the tiger, brain of a flea

Boxing is a risky sport, not least for the fans. What punter doesn't know the pain of saving up for months and queuing for hours in order to be ringside at the big fight—only to be back in their car three minutes later, because some chump hit the canvas.

There were quite a few poorer but wiser sports fans in Michigan in 1997 after Crawford 'the Terminator' Grimsley showed his stuff. His stuff involved getting hit on the chin within 1.7 seconds, then lying down on the canvas for a further ten. That's all, folks. Please take your bags and leave.

But probably the most disappointing performance in boxing history came courtesy of one Daniel Caruso. Moments before his first bout, at the 1992 Golden Gloves Championship in New York, this deeply amateur amateur wanted to show the crowd that he was psyched for the fight. So he punched himself a few times in the face.

Result? He broke his own nose, couldn't stop the bleeding and the doctor declared him unfit to fight.

Big Frank Bruno

A brave journalist will go anywhere for a story, be it a warzone where the fighting is thickest, or a humanitarian disaster where there are no restaurants for miles. It takes a particularly brave journalist, however, to venture into a boxer's bathroom in the moments just after a fight—large, sweaty, naked men are a sight best left unseen.

One such fearless newshound was at the Royal Albert Hall in 1985, however, when Frank Bruno defeated Larry Frazier in the second round. Anxious for a scoop, he dashed downstairs to the change rooms and caught big Bruno stark naked, coming out of the showers.

'What do you plan to do next?' asked the reporter, all business, pen in hand and gleam in eye.

'Hopefully dry myself and get some clothes on,' replied the champ.

'Don't you feel it's time you were exposed to somebody in the top ten, so we can see what you're really made of?'

'Well, if you don't know now, nobody will,' said the big boxer, glancing down.

Mope a dope

One of boxing's time-honoured tricks is the old-fashioned rope-a-dope. Boxer A appears listless and hurt, allowing Boxer B to trap him against the ropes. Punch, punch, punch. Ouch, ouch, ouch. Then, wham, the tables are turned. Boxer A suddenly wakes up and starts punching away, taking full advantage of B's tired arms.

At a 1997 heavyweight title fight in Las Vegas, observers thought they were seeing a dope get roped. Former champ Oliver 'The Atomic Bull' McCall was acting more like a comic cow—dropping his gloves, gazing vacantly at the crowd, and wandering around the ring aimlessly, seemingly unable to fight. He barely even seemed to notice that a puzzled 107 kilogram man was pounding his face.

'How cunning,' thought the watching connoisseurs. 'How subtle. He's taking the rope-a-dope to a whole new level.'

At least, that's what they thought up until the end of the fourth round, when McCall made his way to his corner, and began to quietly weep. 'It was easily,' one observed noted, 'one of the top 1,790,502 emotional breakdowns Las Vegas has ever produced.'

The challenger

Muhammad Ali may have been 'The Greatest' but Joe Louis was the best. The longest-reigning heavyweight champion of all time, Louis saw off 25 challengers over 13 years and won 69 of his 72 fights.

Far more memorable, though, was the *way* he won them: with blindingly fast combinations. Two seconds was all it took for Joe's right hand to jab your heart, liver and ribcage, while his left got your nose and your jaw. It wasn't so much 'blink and you'll miss it' as 'blink and you may well die'.

Naturally, this kind of thing tended to put off opponents—even suicidal boxers refused to fight him, thinking that there surely must be an easier way. So a Kansas City fight promoter was quite surprised one day to hear a man ask for a shot at the champ.

'Just let me in there with him. I'll do my best,' the young buck declared, eyes ablaze with the light of battle.

'And what is your best?'

'One hundred yards in ten seconds.'

Julius the journeyman

Winning isn't everything, according to many sportsmen—they also want to make lots of money. In 2011, according to *Forbes* magazine, tennis player Roger Federer earned around $52 million. This puts him slightly behind basketballer LeBron James at $53 million, while both athletes lag behind Tiger Woods, who raked in a cool $58 million. Leading the pack, however, is the Filipino boxer Manny Pacquiao: he's got $67 million more to spend than he did 12 months ago. There's a lot of money to be made if you're good.

There's also money to make if you're bad. Witness the case of Julius Francis, a flabby, aging journeyman who was scheduled to fight 'Iron' Mike Tyson in the year 2000. If you've never heard of Francis, you're not alone. Even his mother is probably a bit hazy.

Suffice to say, Julius was given *no* chance of lasting three minutes against the champ, who had 20 first-round knockouts to his credit. Punters would, the *Daily Mirror* felt sure, be seeing the soles of Francis's feet more than his right and left hook.

So the paper gave him £200,000 pounds. For advertising space on his soles.

Keeping it nice

'Treat your enemy with courtesy' is an ancient rule of warfare. When the battle's on, you can hack his arm off and make him eat it, then cut a hole in his stomach so he can do it again. But when the battle's over, chivalry begins. The true knight bows before his foe, or at least shakes his remaining hand.

The code of conduct is much the same in boxing, a more modern form of warfare. Sure, Mike Tyson once threatened to eat an opponent's children, but that was (probably) just a bit of fun. When Smokin' Joe Frazier died, for example, his great rival Muhammad Ali couldn't have been kinder. 'The world has lost a great champion,' declared Ali. 'I will always remember Joe with respect and admiration.'

Joe himself, however, didn't always extend his opponents the same courtesy.

'Hey man, what you been doing?' he once greeted a former rival at a social function.

'My wife just had a baby.'

'Congratulations! Whose is it?'

The confident Mr Campbell

Self-belief goes a long way in sport. What the mind believes, the body can do, as psychologists are always telling us. There is a fine line, however, between having a healthy splash of self-belief and drowning in a flood of arrogance. Soccer star Cristiano Ronaldo may just conceivably have crossed it: 'The fans jeer me because I'm good-looking, rich and a great player,' he once said.

Nate Campbell could have also done with a bit more humility the time he fought Robbie Peden for a shot at the World Super Lightweight title. Easily the superior boxer, Campbell dominated the fight for the first five rounds, then decided that it was time to put on a bit of a show. He pranced and he danced and he twirled and he swirled. At one point he even went right up to his wounded opponent, pointed to his chin and then dropped his hands, as if to invite Peden to take a free shot.

So Peden did. Campbell was knocked out with a huge left hook, and stayed knocked out for the rest of the fight.

Iron Mike

If there was ever a bad guy of boxing, it was 'Iron' Mike Tyson. In and out of prison since the age of 12, his rap sheet includes convictions for rape, assault, extortion, road rage, drag racing, possession and DUI. 'I'm just a dark shadowy figure from the bowels of iniquity,' that sweetheart once said. 'I just have this thing inside me that wants to eat and conquer . . . I just want to conquer people and their souls.'

These are not necessarily qualities you'd look for in a son-in-law, but in a boxer, they can't be beat. And nor could Mike for a while there. The youngest ever world heavyweight champion at 20, he is still ranked number one in the ESPN.com list of The Hardest Hitters in Heavyweight History. He was also a pretty hard biter, famously biting off and spitting out the top of Evander Holyfield's ear.

This sort of thing didn't make him very popular with the media, however, and the hostility was very much mutual. 'I wish that you guys had children so I could kick them in the head or stomp on their testicles,' Tyson once told some journalists. 'I'm just a sucker even talking to you guys. I should be ready to rip your heads off your necks.'

On one occasion, Mike was particularly annoyed by a critical column written by Wallace Matthews. 'He called me a rapist and a recluse,' complained the outraged boxer. 'I'm not a recluse!'

SOCCER MOMENTS

Soccer is a game in which a handful of fit men run around for one-and-a-half hours watched by millions of people who could really use the exercise.

Anonymous

Bonding with Sir Alf

The first rule of a professional football career is get on well with the coach. This is also the second, third and fourth rule, while the fifth one involves charming his wife.

The English soccer player Rodney Marsh never quite got this rule—or so, at least, he likes to joke. While the striker had a distinguished club career during the 1960s playing for Fulham and Manchester City, he only managed to make nine international appearances under England coach, Alf Ramsey.

The official explanation for this was that Marsh's retentive style of play didn't fit with the national team's flowing brand of football—and that's probably also the true one. Marsh's explanation, however, is that he never quite connected with the prim and proper Sir Alf, and received a nasty warning just before his ninth match: 'I'll be watching you for the first 45 minutes, Marsh, and if you don't work harder, I'll pull you off at half-time.'

'Crikey, Alf,' a surprised striker replied. 'At Manchester City all we get is an orange and a cup of tea.'

He never played for England again.

A taxi ride in Tottenham

Picture a jackal and a hyena being eaten by sharks while a group of rats stab them all in the back. There in a nutshell you have the Premier League transfer system, English soccer's annual celebration of money and greed. Riven with deceit and betrayal, it is a tough business to be in. Players will insist they're not leaving a club when their contracts are signed and sealed. Agents will solemnly promise they're only dealing with one club when the actual number's more like 42.

Still, life goes on. The only club that could be forgiven for really holding a grudge long after the transfer period is Tottenham Hotspur. In 1997, the smallish club tried to arrange a transfer deal with Monaco's Manu Petit. They flew him out from Monaco, put him up in a swanky hotel, paid all his expenses, and generally wined, dined and wooed. After their final meeting, Hotspur spirits were high: the board was confident it had got its man.

Petit seemed upbeat too, and told the assembled Tottenham board that he just needed to take a drive in order to clear his head. The club happily gave him a taxi chit for a drive around London at their expense. Petit took the taxi down the road to Arsenal, where he signed a deal worth £2.5 million.

He then used his taxi chit to return to Tottenham's headquarters, and give them the bad news.

The Old Firm

To say that Celtic and Rangers 'don't like each other' would be like saying that Batman and the Joker didn't really get on. Collectively known as the Old Firm, Scotland's two most successful clubs don't just represent rival cities, they represent very different demographics: Irish–Scots Catholics in the case of the Celtics, Irish Protestants for the Rangers. The supporters of each club hate the other with the sort of pure, flame-like intensity that the rest of us reserve for mass murderers and people who go on reality TV.

The players aren't immune to this either. On one famous occasion before an Old Firm game, both teams were lined up alongside each other in a tunnel, waiting to hit the pitch. To pass the time, a Rangers defender named John Greig asked the Celtic midfielder Bertie Auld what kind of bonus his team got when they won.

'A fiver,' Auld replied.

'We're on a tenner at Rangers,' Greig immediately boasted.

'Aye, but ours is guaranteed.'

Masturbation in Peru

'It's very strange,' a Peruvian soccer club official once reflected. 'Everyone in Britain seems to think we have a funny name.' Perhaps this is because they do. Founded in 1996, and named after an indigenous tribe of the region, Deportivo Wanka are a struggling second division club that for some reason sells a lot of T-shirts in London.

The fashion industry is fickle, however, and stiff competition in the world of masturbation-related soccer jerseys has recently come from a Swiss outfit called Young Boys Berne—which used to play at Wankdorf Stadium.

In this crowded marketplace, who can say what fate will befall the jerseys of Wankie FC, a little known Zimbabwean club? Perhaps it would be a good marketing move to organise a match with the Indonesian outfit, Semen Padang?

The star recruit

There are two ways to get into the English Premier League. The first is practice, practice and more practice. Get up at dawn, spend all day training, then go to bed early so you can do it again.

The second way involves prank phone calls. This was the method pioneered by one Ali Dia, a Senegalese soccer player who'd worked his way around some of the lowest level soccer leagues in Europe and been kicked out of every one for being terrible. In 1996, he had a friend ring up the manager of Southampton and pretend to be George Weah, Liberian international and former FIFA World Player of the Year. Weah told the manager that Dia was his cousin and had played for the Senegalese national team.

'I'll take him,' said the delighted manager, a quick decision maker, if not a very good one.

Dia turned up at training on the Friday and was selected to play on the Saturday, despite having rather failed to shine. 'Our jaws all dropped to the floor,' team mate Matt Le Tissier later recalled.

On game day, Le Tissier went on, Dia's 'performance was almost comical . . . He was just wandering everywhere. I don't think he realised what position he was supposed to be in. I don't even know if he spoke English.'

Two weeks after the one and only match Dia played, he was released from his Southampton contract.

The master criminal

Some sportspeople are less than bright. Take the quarter-back who sent a picture of his genitals to a model in the hope of impressing her (it didn't). Or the basketballer who tried to smuggle marijuana through the metal detector at an airport—by wrapping it in aluminium foil. And then you have the Brazilian striker who tried to treat a blood blister under his toenail by popping it with a power drill.

But perhaps it's unfair to just single out people who play sport. People who *watch* sport can be pretty dumb too. Take the criminal mastermind who attacked and robbed a German football fan in 2006. Rifling through her purse, the soccer-loving scoundrel discovered a ticket for a World Cup football match that afternoon—so he turned up at the game and took her seat.

Strangely enough, he found himself sitting next to the fan's husband, who had been patiently waiting for his wife to arrive. A couple of quick phone calls later, the crim was sitting inside a cell.

The Lord is their shepherd

Christians like to say that God is everywhere—and when it comes to soccer, they're right. Every second player seems to wear a crucifix these days or have some kind of religious statement tattooed on their wrist. After they beat Argentina in 2005, a bunch of Brazilian players even ripped off their jerseys to reveal T-shirts reading 'Jesus Loves You' in several languages.

On one occasion, the devout Brazilian goalkeeper Senhor Isadore Irandir knelt in front of his goal for a quick prayer to God pre-match. He was still going when the whistle sounded, so opposition player Roberto Rivelino promptly booted the ball from the halfway line and managed to score a goal.

Equally devout was a Croatian defender whose name was Goran Granic. When that shin-crunching hard man saw the light, he decided to completely change his style of play. 'God would not like players to commit harsh fouls,' he claimed.

The change was not well received by fans of his club, Hajduk Split, the reigning Croatian champions, who were cruelly eliminated from the Champions League after Granic put in a soft defensive effort. 'I could probably have saved some key goals,' he admitted afterwards, 'if I had committed fouls to stop players scoring.'

The chicken and the flapper

The Mindil Beach Social Ice Hockey team are unbeatable. Based in Darwin, a city without an ice hockey rink, they gather at a park every Saturday night and wait for all the top clubs from around the world to accept their invitation to play a match. So far, none of them ever have, so Mindil wins every match by forfeit.

Another unbeatable team was Manchester United in the mid-1960s—though Liverpool manager Bill Shankly begged to disagree. While he was addressing his boys before a match between the great rivals, Shankly went through the Man U team sheet, and ridiculed every name that he saw. 'Alex Stepney: a flapper of a goalkeeper. Hands like a Teflon frying pan—nonstick. Right back, Shay Brennan. Slow on the turn, give him a roasting. Left back is Tony Dunne. Even slower than Brennan . . . Paddy Crerand, now he's a deceptive little [bleep]. Slower than he looks!'

And so Shankly demolished the opposing players: 'David Sadler. Wouldn't get a place in our reserves. And finally, John Aston. A chicken, hit him once and you'll never hear from him again.'

Good stuff, very confidence building—but one player wanted to hear more. 'That's all very well, boss,' said Emlyn Hughes, 'but you haven't said anything about George Best, Bobby Charlton or Denis Law.'

The cold Shankly eye turned on him. 'Are you trying to tell me that you can't beat a team that's only got three players in it?'

The love of the game

'Guys aren't able to get $15 million or $20 million any more,' the former NBA star Anfernee Hardaway once said, 'so you have to play for the love of the game.' Unfortunately, not all sports stars are as down to earth as Anfernee. Some players seem to see their sports careers as just a way of amassing money. They don't play for the love of the jumper so much as for the luxuries a big win can bring.

Alan Wright probably doesn't fall into this category. The former Aston Villa soccer player seems like a decent bloke. Nevertheless, most ordinary Englishmen probably found it hard to feel *that* happy for the five foot four inch defender when he splashed out £500,000 on a state-of-the-art Ferrari.

The ordinary Englishmen cheered up a bit later, though; the tiny Wright strained his right knee trying to reach the accelerator, and was forced to trade his Ferrari in for a Rover.

Old-fashioned value

I don't know whether soccer players are a lot better these days, but they're certainly a lot more expensive. In Europe, it's not uncommon for a middling second division player to fetch a multimillion pound transfer fee.

And those sorts of deals pale into insignificance when you consider the prices typically paid for top players. In 2009, for example, Real Madrid purchased Cristiano Ronaldo for £80 million and then Kaká for a further £56 million. Even the so-called 'bargains' like Alan Shearer—who famously cost Blackburn just £3.3 million—aren't exactly what my grandma would call cheap.

To find a true bargain, managers and scouts should travel to Romania, where old-fashioned value is king. Take the tall Romanian defender Marius Cioara. He was sold by second division side UTA Arad to Regal Hornia for 15 kilograms of meat.

'We had to give up the team's sausage allowance for a week to secure him,' a spokesman for Regal Hornia commented, 'but we are confident it will be worth it.'

Job security

According to a US Secret Service maxim, 'society is only four meals away from anarchy'. But this still makes society pretty stable compared to the life of a coach: he's only ever one match away from getting sacked. Sports history is a graveyard of unwanted coaches: men and women who gave their all to their club only to be told 'go away, we want someone else'.

Soccer seems particularly prone to coach-swapping. The London club Queens Park Rangers, for example, has gone through nine managers in the last two-and-a-half years, while clubs like Swansea, Crystal Palace and Scunthorpe have all ditched coaches within their first week. In 2012, the manager of Brazil's XV de Jau football club was fired just 48 hours into his new role after a 3–1 loss to Flamengo.

But that's a distinguished career compared to Leroy Rosenior's. He was appointed boss of the struggling Torquay United FC at 3.30pm on 17 May 2007, and immediately called a press conference. At 3.40pm, the club was sold to a venture capital firm. Their first order of business was to sack the coach.

C'mon Aussie

Australia is a nation of athletes. We punch above our weight in nearly every sport. To punch above our weight in soccer, however, we'd need to weigh about half a kilogram when fully clothed, then strip off before we got on the scales. Having qualified for three World Cups in 82 years, the Socceroos aren't a joke, precisely, but this is only because they're so bad it's not funny.

In 1980, fresh from a loss to Kuwait, and gearing up for a loss to New Zealand, the Socceroos had just appointed a new coach. Being blessed with eyesight, the new coach could see that the team had big problems with its passing and dribbling, so he asked a colleague for some suggestions.

'We have one training technique which seems to bring results,' the colleague replied. 'We place 11 dustbins in formation on the pitch and have the team practise dribbling and passing around them. Why don't you try it?'

So try it the new coach did.

'How'd it go?' asked his colleague a few days later.

'Not too good. The dustbins beat the Socceroos 3–2.'

A man of his word

If coaching has a cockroach, his name is Tommy 'the Doc' Docherty—Tommy's career just couldn't be killed. The manager of 14 different soccer teams over 31 years and the winner of, um, one cup, his career is a monument to persistence and the importance of being good at job interviews.

Perhaps this is a little unfair: Docherty did have some damn good years. But he is also remembered for leading Queens Park Rangers to last place in the second division, and getting sacked from Manchester United for sleeping with the club physio's wife. After Old Trafford he went back to Queens Park, where he managed to get sacked twice in 1980. He later went on to coach Preston North End, where he lasted two months before getting sacked. Wolverhampton Wanderers then snapped him up, but sacked him again after he masterminded a 21-match losing streak.

But whether or not he could coach, the Doc was a man of integrity. He always kept his word. As he pointed out shortly after being sacked from Rotherham United, 'I promised the chairman I'd get them out of the second division and I did.

'I took them into the third.'

You are what you eat

The modern athlete's diet is specially designed for peak performance. You are what you eat, as the doctors tell us, and most sportspeople are a mix of lean meats and complex carbohydrates, plus fibrous vegetables for a slow release of glucose in the digestive tract and thus a slow release of energy during competition.

Releases from the players' digestive tracts also played a role in a 1902 soccer game between Liverpool and Stoke City—though their lower intestines presumably saw some action as well. The Stoke City players had all dined on fish that lunchtime, and trouble stirred in bowel country almost straightaway. The goalkeeper left the ground within minutes, soon to be followed by a further six players.

'The dressing room resembled the cabin of a cross-Channel steamer in bad weather, and smelt like it . . . only more so,' the doctor later reported. The referee reported a scorecard of 7–0.

David Beckham, thinker

The Manchester United manager Sir Alex Ferguson, said one of his star players at the time, 'is the best manager I've ever had at this level'. A thoughtful pause followed this statement, accompanied by a furrowed brow. You could almost hear the great brain ticking. 'Well actually,' David Beckham finally added, 'he's the only manager I've ever had at this level. But he's the best I ever had.'

Welcome to the mind of one of England's greatest ever midfielders—a man who once announced that he was planning to get his first-born son christened, 'though we don't know which religion yet'.

The nature of genius, of course, is that it can be wayward. Over the course of his career, Beckham has been attacked for criticising referees and causing one or two deliberate fouls. He indignantly rejected a journalist's suggestion that he was a 'volatile' player, however.

'I can play in the centre, on the right, and occasionally on the left side.'

A Great World Cup Moment

Britain's Channel 4 once asked the public to vote for the 100 Greatest World Cup Moments. From Pelé and Maradona to Beckenbauer and Cruyff, some truly great names appear in their final list—not to mention some truly great tackles and extraordinary goals.

The English striker James 'Greavsie' Greaves also features in this glorious pantheon—though this honour pleases him less than you might just think. Greavsie's great World Cup moment occurred in a 1962 quarter-final against Brazil, when a stray black dog managed to run onto the pitch.

Showing admirable presence of mind, the player scooped up said canine and made his way to a steward—only to feel the warm, damp dribble of urine making its slow way down his shirt. 'Maybe the dog thought, "Here's another poor sod who's in just as desperate straits as I am,"' the striker later reflected.

'I smelt so bad, it was awful. I should have won the game for England, because no Brazilian defenders came near me.'

Hull v Hull

Soccer has many great rivalries, epic sagas that live on in legend and song: Liverpool and Man United; Barcelona and Real Madrid; AC and Inter Milan. Every match between those teams is an exciting new chapter in a classic book.

Soccer also has some slightly less great rivalries, which are nevertheless good fun. A case in point can be found in Hull. This small English town has two small English teams, Hull FC and Hull KR—and, naturally enough, they hate each other. Show a Hull FC supporter the red and white jersey of Hull KR and chances are he'll wince with disgust. Show a KR supporter the black and white of FC and it will very probably get covered in vomit.

The clubs' chairmen have always embraced the rivalry, as a 1980 radio interview showed. 'Why is it,' an FC supporter provocatively asked KR chairman Bill Land, 'that Hull FC get 10,000 supporters for a home game and Hull KR get only 5000 supporters for a home game?'

'Well, son, I will have to refer you to the bible to answer that question,' Mr Land replied. 'It says in the good book that for every wise man there are two fools.'

Coulda, woulda, shoulda

Sport is full of couldabeens—men and women who could have made the big time, if not for some cast-iron excuse. Whether it was school commitments that meant they couldn't go to training, or an injury that cut them off in their prime, every pub has a sporting superstar who for some reason became an accountant instead.

Actual sporting superstars get to meet them all the time. The former Celtic striker Charlie Nicholas was no exception here. A man with more than just talent to burn, he was minding his own business in a bar one day when a drunken Rangers fan got in his face.

'Charlie, Charlie, you're nae better than me,' he slurred. 'I could have made it . . . What can y' dae that I cannae?'

Ever so calmly, Charlie got out a matchbox and proceeded to burn a £50 note. 'That!' he said, and walked away.

Love hurts

A team of Harvard University scientists has discovered that after men get married their testosterone tends to plummet. This discovery may have interesting implications for sport. Many fans believe in the 'marriage curse'—the idea that a sportsman's form always slinks away the moment he walks down the aisle. Could lower testosterone levels mean this is true?

Well, recent tennis history bears this out to some degree—Sampras, Agassi, McEnroe and Borg were all number one when they married, only to immediately see their ranking slide—but the only sportsman that scientists can conclusively say suffered from his marriage is a Portuguese soccer player named Paulo Diogo.

In 2004, Diogo scored a goal and tried to jump over a fence to celebrate with the fans, only he got his wedding ring caught on the fence. As a result, he got a yellow card for wasting time . . . and doctors had to amputate what remained of his finger.

Goalweepers

Question: What do you call someone who hangs out with soccer players?

Answer: A goalkeeper—*boom tish*!

It's just a fact that goalkeepers don't require as much skill as the rest of the players in their team. I mean, take a look at this list of goalkeeper injuries and tell me how much skill these blokes must have:

- Stalybridge's Mark Statham trapped his head in a car door.
- Liverpool's Michael Stensgaard hurt his shoulder setting up an ironing board.
- Chelsea's Carlo Cudicini damaged a knee reaching for a remote control.
- Everton's Richard Wright twisted his ankle during a warm up by falling over a sign that warned players not to warm up in that area.
- Valencia's Santiago Canizares dropped cologne on his foot and severed a tendon.
- Wimbledon's Dave Beasant dropped a jar of mayonnaise on his foot and broke his big toe.

Sherlock Pickles

Even when England won the World Cup, they managed to lose it too. In 1966, the old country was due to host soccer's most important tournament. The cup itself—the gold-plated, solid silver Jules Rimet Trophy—was sent to England for display a few months before the tournament, as a special favour from FIFA authorities. Borrowing the cup took weeks of painstaking negotiation and England's categorical assurance that every security measure would be taken.

As it happened, however, they forgot one measure: security. The trophy was stolen from a public exhibition while the security guards were on a break. Rather embarrassing for all concerned.

For the next week, Scotland Yard's finest scoured the country using the very latest forensic techniques. They found nothing. It took a Thames River barge worker to save the country's pride—or rather, it took his dog, Pickles. Out for a walk with his owner one morning, Pickles began digging away under a hedge and, whammo, look what he found.

England went on to win the tournament that year—but without Pickles there'd have been no World Cup.

The lighter side of brain damage

Over 2000 American football players recently filed a lawsuit against the NFL, accusing it of concealing research that associates concussion with long-term brain damage or depression. A few former Australian Rules footballers have also come forward in recent years, claiming to have had concussion-related health problems post career.

Consequently, sports teams have started taking knocks to the head and concussion more seriously. Concussed athletes now tend to be evaluated by a doctor before they return to the field.

Most sports teams are taking it seriously, anyway. Back in the 1990s, a striker for Glasgow soccer club Partick Thistle got hit in the head during a game. He was so concussed, club trainers told the coach, he didn't even know who he was.

'That's great. Tell him he's Pelé and get him back on.'

GOLF
MOMENTS

Golf is played by twenty million mature American men whose wives think they are out having fun.

Jim Bishop

The accurate Mr Nelson

If a golfer mis-hits a ball and sends it hurtling towards your head, he's supposed to yell out, 'Fore!' Generally, of course, he doesn't manage to find the time, being too busy saying 'shit!' The word is thought to derive from 'fore-caddy'—an additional caddy that golfers used to hire sometimes to stand where they were aiming, to make sure they didn't lose a ball. When their aim was dangerously good, they'd yell out 'Fore-caddy!' to warn him, and the word was eventually shortened to 'fore'.

Fore-caddies were still pretty common in the 1930s, especially on the practice range. The PGA golfer Byron Nelson often used one, but it seems that once, when practising with a two-iron, he foolishly forgot to yell 'Fore'. Whack. Ouch. Thud.

Now, a good two-iron can go about 190 metres, so hitting your 'marker' is no mean feat. 'You must have been an unbelievably accurate long-iron player, Mr Nelson,' the golfer was later told by an adoring fan.

'Sure was. I hit him another six times before he got up.'

Such praise

The most famous name in American golf really ought to be Donald Ross. Sure, Jack Nicklaus won a few tournaments, and Tiger Woods can hit a bit, but the golf industry as a whole owes much more to the man who designed over 400 courses. The 'patron saint of American golf architecture', Ross's timelessly challenging courses have hosted 21 US Opens, 15 PGA Championships, 11 Women's Amateurs and five Ryder Cups.

His most famous course is Pinehurst No. 2 in North Carolina. Considered by Ross to be 'the fairest test of championship golf I ever designed', the iconic Pinehurst hosted its first professional tournament in 1940. Ben Hogan, one of the big names of the day, won it, and Ross cabled him saying, 'Excellent. The greatest.'

'Undeserving of such praise,' a modest Hogan cabled back.

'I meant the course.'

'So did I.'

'Thunder' Bolt

'Here's irony for you,' a notoriously bad-tempered golfer once remarked. 'The driver goes the shortest distance when you throw it. The putter flies farthest, followed by the sand wedge.'

That golfer was 'Terrible Tempered' Tommy 'Thunder' Bolt, and in such matters his word was law. 'Never break your driver and your putter in the same round,' was another one of Thunder Bolt's mottos, while he once advised a young Arnold Palmer to 'always throw your clubs ahead of you. That way, you won't waste energy going back to pick them up.'

More famous for being thrown out of tournaments than he was for actually winning them, Bolt was once reported by two female spectators for using (gasp!) an 'obscenity'. An official handed Thunder a $100 fine, but the golfer was quick to protest. Where was this swear word supposedly uttered? Bolt asked. Surely I am innocent until you've proven guilt?

So the official took him to the spot where the incident had occurred, in the hope of jogging his memory. Seeing it, Bolt promptly handed over $300, so he could utter the swear word two more times.

Harpo and the heat

Golf is God's gift to the stickler. It's a game with thousands of petty little rules, and the true golf pedant knows them all. He might miss all his putts, or have a dreadful day with the driver, but give the pedant just one chance to penalise your drop out of a water hazard, and he'll go home a happy man. Give him a chance to cite the dress code, and he'll probably have an orgasm.

A golf pedant once got such an opportunity at LA's Hillcrest Country Club on a swelteringly hot summer day. The comedians Harpo Marx and George Burns were playing a round and, it being so hot, they decided to take off their tops.

'Shirts must be worn at all times,' the pedant piped up, after roughly 0.000006 seconds had passed.

'Why?' the comedians replied. 'We can go to a public beach without them.'

'Rules are rules. You can't play without a shirt.'

Reluctantly, Harpo and George put their shirts back on—then, after a quiet word, they took off something else.

'It says we can't play without shirts. But show me the rule that says we can't play without pants.'

The efficient golfer

The American business world is full of go-getters, men who can do because they know how. They're up bright and early to get themselves to the gym, then hit the desk a bit before dawn. Several important meetings later, it's time for a power lunch, so they can cut a few big deals during the afternoon. Come 8pm, they head off to dinner and the opera or perhaps for a quick romp with their blonde new secretary. Then it's back home to drink some scotch and criticise their wife and kids.

This kind of hectic schedule doesn't leave much room for golf, but some moguls still find the time. The Hollywood producer Louis B Mayer, for example, insisted on squeezing the occasional round into his schedule, as he thought that proficiency at the game gave one a certain class. He never quite became proficient, however, consistently scoring in the hundreds.

But by employing two caddies so he could find his balls quicker, Mayer did manage to be *efficient* instead. Whenever a game finished, it's said, he'd consult his watch, rather than the scorecard. 'We made it in one hour and seven minutes! Three minutes better than yesterday!'

Stuck in the cart

Once, it's said, the golfer Phil Boulton was playing a pro–am at a flash new course by the South China Sea. His amateur playing partner was a young Australian guy named Johnny, who had been allocated a beautiful Chinese girl as his caddy for the tournament. He was the envy of every other player.

But maybe he shouldn't have been. The beautiful caddy kept touching the young amateur on his hand when he was selecting his clubs, and it seemed to make the young player very nervy. When they came to the 13th hole, a short par three, everyone hit their shots except Johnny. Oddly reluctant to get out of the golf cart, he sat there next to his caddy, who was ever so softly stroking his hand.

After a minute or two, a Chinese official approached the player and told him that the time had come when he had to hit. Reluctantly, Johnny rose from the cart and— standing a little hunched over—awkwardly addressed the ball. His shot flew well over the green and landed in a distant bunker.

Phil Boulton smiled. 'You were stiff there, mate.'

Don't mess with the Tetherington

While golf, it has been noted, was originally restricted to wealthy, overweight Protestants, it's now open to anybody who owns hideous clothing. This is undoubtedly a good thing from the point of view of democracy, and presumably a boon for makers of lemon-coloured trousers. But it's been terrible news for car parking.

The comedian Ronnie Corbett once related a story about a golfer named John Tetherington. It seems that this wealthy Mercedes driver was stuck outside the course for half an hour one day as he looked high and low for a car park. Eventually, at long last, he found a space, and duly pulled up alongside it, all ready to reverse his car in.

He wasn't ready for treachery, however. At the last moment, some brightly trousered young punk drove nose first straight into the vacant spot and jumped out of his car with a cocky wink. 'You've got to be young to do that,' he quipped.

Young and dumb. Furious, Tetherington stepped on the pedal and slammed straight into the man's car.

'And you've got to be wealthy to do that!' he said.

Lost in translation

International business can be conducted in boardrooms, in restaurants or over the phone. More and more frequently, however, it's being conducted on the golf course—a place where anyone, regardless of creed or colour, can hack, shank and slice just like everyone else.

Golf has proved a particularly useful entrée into the business culture of Japan. The country is full of high-powered executives who spend all their time fretting about their short game, or trying to work out how exactly one putts. Professional golf coaches are often sent there at the behest of large companies to supply golf tips and general goodwill.

One Australian pro was on such a mission a few years ago on behalf of a prominent motor company. The executive the pro was instructing had more than just his short game to worry about, however: pretty much every shot he hit sucked. On the 16th, though, he finally struck gold—or at least struck a ball that went long and straight.

'Furokku! Furokku!' the pro cried out, after searching his mind for a term meaning 'great shot'.

The next day he had to search for another job. Turns out that 'furokku' means 'fluke'.

A good round gone bad

One morning at Yarra Bend Golf Club in 1986, a legend was born. No one knows the bloke's name, but his deeds are spoken of in hushed tones over cold beers in clubhouses all over the country.

It was a Saturday competition, and the golfer was having a blinder. He was ten shots better than his handicap as he came to the 16th hole, a tame par four with a giant bunker at the front and the Yarra River a little way to the left. But over the following, um, 14 strokes, he saw quite a lot of that bunker. Then he chipped the ball into the river.

Calmly, the golfer placed his putter in his bag, strolled over to the Yarra River—and threw the whole bag in. He then strolled off in the direction of the car park, leaving several stunned onlookers in his wake.

Five minutes later, however, they saw the man stroll back. He took off his shoes and clothes, waded into the river, and began to dive for his clubs. After three dives down in the murky water, he found the golf set and dragged it out. The man then rummaged through the front pocket of the bag and retrieved his car keys.

And threw the whole set back in the Yarra.

The problem with caddies

Opinion is divided on the subject of caddies, the people who carry a pro's golf clubs and give him advice and support. Some golfers find them annoying. Other golfers find them very annoying. 'I know you can be fined for throwing a club,' the former US Open champ Tommy 'Thunder' Bolt once commented, 'but I want to know if you can get fined for throwing a caddy?'

In part, this distaste is a result of the fact that professional sportspeople can be arrogant. 'If I needed advice from my caddy,' the golfer Bobby Jones once said, 'he'd be hitting the shots and I'd be carrying the bag.'

But it's also because caddies can be a little arrogant themselves. Mike Souchak, a 15-time winner on the PGA tour, was one of many golfers to suffer at a caddy's hands. One day, during an important tournament, it's said he ignored his caddy's advice that he should hit a three-iron—and instead hit a four-wood straight into the hole.

'How's that?' he asked the caddy, triumphantly.

'Not bad, but you'd have done better with a three-iron.'

If at first you don't succeed, fail, fail again

Want to know the secret to success in golf?

So do the rest of us. We all know that it's got something to do with keeping your head over the ball, and your grip soft yet firm. The knees must be slightly—but not *too*—bent, and the club face neither open nor closed. Your swing, the authorities add, must be a full, easy motion, which smoothly progresses from backswing to downswing to follow-through—and don't forget to watch where the ball goes, so you can find it and play your next shot. 'If you watch a game, it's fun and if you play it, it's recreation,' Bob Hope once remarked. 'If you work at it, it's golf.'

One day at St Andrews, the story goes, a despairing American golfer decided that he could work at it no more. Possibly because he'd forgotten to position the middle of shoulders directly over the top of both the knee cap and the ball of the foot, or perhaps because his clubface wasn't parallel to the forearm at the three-quarter mark of his swing, he was having a simply dreadful round—and then he topped it off by hitting his ball in a lake.

Perhaps, said the golfer darkly, he should throw himself in the lake as well.

'No, don't!' protested his caddy. 'You couldn't keep your head down long enough.'

The cruellest game

The difference between golf and tennis, someone once pointed out, is that in tennis you want to kill the other player. In golf you just want to kill yourself. Like life, small children and people who don't like moustaches, the game can be very cruel.

For a start, just look at the rules. If you ask your partner what club he just hit, you get a two-stroke penalty for soliciting information. If you use the green to wipe bird poo off your ball, it's a two-stroke penalty for testing the putting surface. You'll even be penalised strokes if you then fall over and break your ankle, if in doing so you damage the green.

But an even more obnoxious feature of golf is the scoring system: you can wipe out an entire day's good work in 0.4 seconds or less. Every golfer knows what it is to play the round of his life, then lose three balls and miss a putt on the 18th.

Three-time PGA tour winner Stephen Lowery had it even worse. Once, at the 17th hole of one of the richest tournaments in the world, that pro hit a perfect drive. The ball landed right in the centre of the green. The crowd cheered, the player smiled, and all was well with the world.

Then it wasn't. A seagull suddenly descended from the sky, picked up the ball, flew 20 metres into the air—and dropped it right in the middle of a lake.

The immortal

Every golfer, no matter how dreadful, has a highlights reel to rival the best. If you take away all those diabolical four-irons and terrible drives, you're generally left with about five shots. But those five shots are things of beauty: so fluid, so straight, so crisp. It's those occasional good'uns that keep the hack coming back—that make him think, 'I can do this', when all available evidence clearly shows that he can't.

The holy grail of good'uns is, of course, the hole in one. Man blames fate for other accidents, as Martha Beckman once pointed out, but feels personally responsible for one of those.

The comedian Groucho Marx was once personally responsible for a hole in one. Never known to hide his light under a bushel, he was quick to tell the world. *The Boston Globe* even picked up on the story: it ran a photo of Marx between photos of Walter Hagen and Bobby Jones, the biggest golf stars of the day. The photo caption read 'Groucho joins the immortals'.

The next day, Groucho played golf again, under the keen eyes of several reporters. But on the same hole as the previous day's triumph, he shot a somewhat less impressive 21. 'And that was only because I was putting unusually well.' The next day, *The Boston Globe* ran the same visual as the day before, with photos of Hagen and Jones, but there was a blank space where Groucho Marx's photo had been.

The caption? 'Groucho leaves the immortals.'

Stiff upper lip

One of the best things about golf is that it makes every-body, absolutely *everybody*, swear. If Mother Teresa ever muffed an approach shot, she would have said 'shit', not 'whoops'. And when a Buddhist monk gets stuck in a bunker, small children should cover their ears.

Other golfers, of course, do more than just swear. Take the PGA tour winner Woody Austin, who managed to break his putter . . . by smashing it on his own face. Or the US Open champ Tommy 'Thunder' Bolt, who made an art form out of throwing clubs everywhere. On one occasion, he even shook his fist to the heavens, screaming, 'Why don't you come down here and fight like a man?'

All this petulance makes the example of Charles Coody so much more impressive. A winner of the 1971 Masters, and member of the Texan Sports Hall of Fame, Coody had his bad patches like anyone else—but he endured them with a Zen-like calm. 'I'm hitting my drives badly, my iron play is erratic and the putts are just not falling in,' he once told a journalist. 'But other than that, everything is just fine.'

A real problem

'After all, golf is only a game,' said Millicent, a character in a story by PG Wodehouse. 'Women,' the author hastens to add, 'say these things without thinking. It does not mean that there is a kink in their character. They simply don't realise what they are saying.'

But perhaps Wodehouse was being too kind. The former PGA Player of the Year, Sam Snead, for example, can vouch that at least one woman definitely had a kink in her character—and where there's one, there could be more.

'I was over in York, England,' Snead once told *Golf World* magazine, and 'there was this man and his wife. She didn't know how to play golf. She didn't play. And of course, he played a little golf. And they went out to the tournament we were playing in York.

'This professional came up the 18th and he sliced his ball over to the right of the green into the trash. And he hit the ball from the trash into the trap. And from the trap he got it out into the high grass short of the green. So this guy watching says, "Gee, he's having a terrible day."

'From there, the player put it in the hole. And she said, "Well now he's got a real problem."'

A mental exercise

Stephen Coverdale, the former chief executive of Northamptonshire Cricket Club, is, as you would expect, a busy man. But he still finds time for golf.

During one of these times, he was playing a round with a friend who fancied himself as a bit of a ladies' man. The friend also fancied himself as a bit of a golfer, but in this respect, at least, he was wrong. 'The more he tried, the worse he got and the more his temper increased,' Coverdale recalled.

Eventually, red-faced and furious, the friend managed to hook his ball out of bounds on the 17th hole—and then slice his replacement ball out of bounds after that. Panting and cursing and sweating and muttering, the friend prepared to take another shot—but Coverdale gently intervened.

'Slow down,' he soothingly counselled. 'Take it gently. Imagine you're making love to your secretary.'

'How the hell do you think I can hit a golf ball with a paper bag over my face?'

A room with a few

Life on the road can be tough for sportspeople, and not just because they miss family and friends. For one thing, it's not exactly tourism. Athletes rarely get to see any sights, let alone enjoy the sounds and the smells. If they're in New York, they won't see the Empire State Building; when in London, they miss out on Big Ben. For the professional sportsperson, every city is basically an airport and a hotel room, plus some taxis and a gym.

It's therefore ever so important that their hotel room be OK. When the golfer Lee Trevino played in Australia one year, his, unfortunately, was not. 'The room I have at my hotel is so small that the rats are all round-shouldered,' he joked to a local journo.

But you should never ever joke to a journo: Trevino's one-liner made the news. The manager of the hotel was naturally very upset, so he asked the golfer to issue a public apology at a tournament function that night.

Trevino dutifully did. 'I apologise if I upset anybody today when I said that the rats in this hotel are round-shouldered. They're not.'

Sir Henry's hole

Golf is one of life's great levellers: it keeps millions of egos in check. It doesn't matter how high you rise in society, how much success you keep striking in life—at some stage you'll stuff up an approach shot, or putt a ball so that it shoots off the green. There are so many ways to make a mistake in golf, and most players make them all.

Sir Henry Winneke AC, KCMG, KCVO, OBE, KStJ, QC struck quite a bit of success in life, as you may just have gathered from the letters after his name. But when he wasn't busy being Victoria's Governor and Supreme Court Chief Justice, or a Knight of the Most Venerable Order of St John, that great statesman liked to golf. With a handicap of 16, he was pretty successful at that too—but the game got him in the end.

One day, it's said, Sir Henry hit his ball in the rough, as all golfers sometimes do. Bending over to identify it, he then managed to get hit himself. A female golfer had hit right behind him, and her ball ended up right where it hurt.

'Madam,' said His Excellency reprovingly. 'Would you kindly aim at the hole with the flag in it?'

The stealer-dealer

'Golf,' said Bob Hope, 'is a hard game to figure. One day you will go out and slice it and shank it, hit into all the traps and miss every green. The next day you go out and, for no reason at all, you really stink.'

He did get better, I'm happy to say. The comedian went to his grave with a handicap of four, after playing 2000 courses all over the world. He even used the game to make money for charity, founding the annual Bob Hope Classic.

But he also made money for himself. One day, the story goes, Hope was playing a round with Samuel Goldwyn, a big-shot producer in Hollywood movie circles but a bit of an untouchable on the course. On one hole, Goldwyn took half-a-dozen shots to get to the green and then managed to miss a two-foot putt. Disgusted, he threw away his putter.

Hope quietly put the putter in his bag, and took it out on the very next hole. Bang! He sank a sensational putt.

'Let me see that putter for a minute,' said a thoughtful Goldwyn, and subjected the club to some scrutiny. 'I like this club very much,' he eventually declared. 'Will you sell it to me?'

'Sure, it'll cost you $50.'

Walter and the Chick

Every now and then in sport, there's a changing of the guard. A young up-and-comer arrives on the scene and the aging champ bows gracefully out.

Golf is no exception to this rule. In the 1930s, the biggest name in the game was Walter Hagen, a veteran then in his 40s. But most fans were more excited by Melvin 'Chick' Harbert, a 20-something sensation.

In 1932, the young buck met the old lion in an exhibition match. 'We came to the 18th both needing birdies for 71 and both facing three-metre putts,' Chick later recalled. 'I wanted to beat him so bad I could taste it. I got down on my stomach and lined up the putt. And I lined it up from both sides and looked over it like it was life or death. Then I stepped up and—pop—made the putt.'

'Then I walked over to the side, as if to say, "Well, it's your turn." Hagen then went through *every* motion that I had been through. Exactly. He got down on his stomach and lined it up. Same mannerisms. Then he stepped up—left-handed—and back-handed the ball into the cup.'

A famous victory

Some golfers are known for grabbing an early lead and never letting go, while others enjoy a good choke. The most satisfying sort of golfer, however, belongs in the Arnold Palmer category. They bumble and stumble in the early rounds of a tournament, then charge home to victory on the final day.

Palmer's talents in this regard were never more evident than on the final day of the British Open in 1961. Trudging through swirling winds and torrential rain, he found himself deep in the rough on the 16th hole, and needing to navigate the ball through a narrow gap in order to get on the green. 'It could get through but if it doesn't, it's the end of the game,' Palmer thought to himself—and then he hit the ball to within two feet of the hole, and stormed home to a famous win.

A plaque now marks that spot on the 16th—and in 1989, when Palmer was practising at Royal Troon, a photographer asked him to pose alongside it. The golfer agreed but, after looking here, there and everywhere on the 16th hole, he couldn't for the life of him find the plaque.

'Tip, where is that plaque?' he irritably asked his caddy.

'About 200 miles south of here, Mr Palmer. It was at Royal Birkdale, not Royal Troon.'

The magic word

The golf bug can bite at any time, even if you're a Hollywood hotshot.

Samuel L Jackson is so stricken with the virus that he even has time out from filming written into his contracts so he can hit the course at least twice a week. With a handicap of eight, the *Pulp Fiction* star can often be seen at celebrity pro–ams, wearing strange pants and signing autographs.

Provided people say 'please', that is. Once, during one such tournament, the actor found himself near a large group of kids, all waving programs for him to sign. 'But I don't hear "please", so I figure it's time to enforce the rules. I announce loudly, so the whole gallery can hear, "What are you supposed to say?" The kids don't answer, they just continue waving the programs.

'I repeat myself, this time more sternly: "What's the magic word?" Still no answer.

'I'm ready to walk away when one of the bigger kids, with a look of total frustration on his face, starts mumbling loudly. Then it hits me. These kids were from a local school for the deaf.'

Tricky Dickie

Richard Nixon knew the difference between right and wrong, he just didn't think it was very important. His fellow former President Harry Truman was actually being quite understated when he noted that 'Nixon is a no good, lying bastard. He can lie out of both sides of his mouth at the same time, and if he ever caught himself telling the truth, he'd lie just to keep his hand in.'

There was certainly no danger of Nixon ever telling the truth on the golf course—at least, not if an anecdote from Sam Snead is anything to go by. Nixon played many rounds during his presidency, and one of them was with the former PGA star. On one hole, Snead later recalled, Tricky Dickie had 'landed in some rough no one could shoot out of unless you had a bazooka. I was watching him from the fairway when he disappeared into a thicket. Hell, I figured he was going to drop another ball, take his loss like anyone else in that situation and play on.

'But hell no—out comes his ball, flyin' high onto the fairway. Then Nixon comes out of the woods looking real pleased with himself. I knew he threw it out, but I didn't say anything.

'What *could* I say? He was the president.'

Little Phil

'If your baby is beautiful and perfect, never cries or fusses, sleeps on schedule and burps on demand and an angel all the time,' someone once said, 'chances are you're the grandparent.' Unfortunately for the parents of golfer Phil Mickelson, they were the parents of golfer Phil Mickelson. And an angel he was not.

One example of these non-angelic tendencies came when the future Masters champ was three-and-a-half and had just discovered the game that would make his name. 'I was begging my dad to take me to play golf,' Mickelson once recalled, but 'he thought I was too young. So I packed my Flopsy stuffed animal and a bunch of balls into a suitcase, put my clubs over my shoulder and ran away.'

But where's a boy to go? Lacking cab money, maps or a sense of direction, little Phil asked his neighbour a few doors down the street to please direct him to the course. 'She knew something was up and told me to take four left turns.

'I did, and when I returned to where I started, which was home, my parents were waiting.'

Aging gracefully

There comes a moment in every sportsperson's life when their aging limbs say, 'Time's up.' And if those limbs don't say it quite loud enough, he or she can generally find a few people who are prepared to speak up instead.

Nick Faldo found one such spokesperson at an international airport. The golfer was in his late 40s at the time and combining his playing career with a bit of commentary on TV. He was getting help filling out his passenger arrival card and in the space under 'occupation', the customs officer wrote the words 'sports analyst'.

'Why not just write "Golfer"?' Faldo asked, ever so slightly peeved. 'What about the six majors?'

'We both know what you do best these days,' the customs officer replied.

Spend and swing

Golf books are the worst; they don't waste your money so much as your time. Not only will you simply never get back the hours you spent studying Ben Hogan's *Modern Fundamentals of Golf* or *How I Play Golf* by Tiger Woods—you will play worse for reading them too. Before you opened the book, you had a clear mind and easy swing, but after you close it, your fuddled brain will never forget the need to play with 'swing planes' or master the art of 'synchronisation'.

In 2007, the PGA coach Stuart Howard was giving a golf lesson to one such golf reader. He tried to keep the lesson simple but it was to no avail. 'What about my lower body coil?' 'Is my clubface parallel?' The man used every technical term under the sun, but hit the ball like an unco giraffe.

Eventually, a frustrated Howard said, 'You know, you're right, here's what you need to do. Keep the club in front of the plain on take away, and hinge laterally and early, then work to a lay-off at the top by a steady pronation of the left arm. Begin the downward plain from no more than parallel, and come from inside the target line, making sure your right-to-left weight transition is synchronised with impact to keep your left side stable.'

Silence.

BASKETBALL
MOMENTS

Basketball is the second most exciting indoor sport, and the other one shouldn't have spectators.

Dick Vertlieb

Charles Barkley, do-gooder

Once upon a time, an NBA player got frustrated, and hurled the ball into the stands. Unsurprisingly, it hit a spectator, who was knocked out and stretchered off. As the camera closed in on the man's little daughter, sobbing helplessly amid the blood, Charles Barkley offered this comment: 'You know why that little girl's crying? It's because she's thinking, "My daddy's a wussy".'

Welcome to the world of Charles Barkley, a basketballer known to fans as 'The Round Mound of Rebound' and to police as a repeat offender. Fond of brawling at nightclubs, Chuck's career highlights include spitting at a spectator and running a red light while under the influence. Though that last offence was fair enough, as he explained to police at the time: he was in a hurry to meet up with a prostitute.

Chuck's biggest legal problems, however, have been those pesky rules about assault and battery. In 1997, he was even forced to go to court just because he'd thrown some guy through a plate glass window.

'Your sanctions are community service and a fine,' said the judge sternly. 'Do you have any regrets?'

Sure do, replied the superstar: 'I regret we weren't on a higher floor.'

Democracy in LA

Once upon a time, joining a team was tough. A new recruit's initiation generally involved getting their head shoved down the toilet, or being made to hitchhike in the nude. Nowadays, however, the club environment is all about consultation and communication; about making people feel like they're valued members of the team. 'Treat players with respect, and you will earn their respect', goes the modern leader's mantra.

A former captain of the LA Lakers kind of subscribed to this philosophy. While Elgin Baylor believed in empowering his players, he never got carried away. One year, for example, when the team was due to get a new uniform, he agreed to take a vote on whether the blazers should be blue or gold.

The players voted for gold but a few weeks later, when the blazers arrived, they turned out to be blue. 'I told 'em I'd give 'em the vote,' Baylor explained to a colleague. 'I didn't say I'd count it.'

When Orlando lost its Magic

While 93.482% of statistics are completely made up, a few are actually true. One of the more interesting ones comes from German sports psychologists at the University of Munster: they say that teams in red tops win more often. Whether they be playing soccer, football or taekwondo, the theory is that red gives competitors more confidence, and makes opponents see them as aggressive and dominant.

A less surprising statistic is that teams tend to play better at home. A supportive crowd, familiar surroundings, and not having to travel all help to give the home team an advantage. This advantage seems to be particularly marked in the NBA—perhaps because the backboards are made of glass, which lets home fans shake objects to distract visiting players when they try to score. But at the midway point of 1991, the once formidable Orlando Magic had lost 27 games for just seven wins.

'We can't win at home, we can't win on the road,' said the despondent coach, Pat Williams. 'As general manager, I just can't figure out where else to play.'

Being is believing

To be your best, you've got to believe you're the best, according to one school of thought. Confidence is *everything*. Even a lack of talent can be overcome.

A former coach of the Chicago Bulls was one of many subscribers to this philosophy. Johnny Kerr's team had a bit of an inferiority complex, and it was one that was well deserved. So before a game against the all-conquering Boston Celtics—a team that was fully expected to conquer the Bulls—Kerr asked his forwards to close their eyes for a moment and pretend that they were the best. He told his starting centre to pretend that he was the NBA's best starting centre, and his defensive guards to tell themselves that they could run their defence better than any other players around.

It didn't work—the Bulls were thrashed.

'Don't worry about it, coach,' said one of the players afterwards. 'Just pretend we won.'

Silence please

Once upon a time, two NBA basketball referees were taking a walk through the countryside, when they came across some unfamiliar tracks. 'Deer tracks?' proposed the first ref, a little tentatively. 'No, bear tracks,' suggested the second. There followed a few more minutes of discussion, which ended when they were hit by a train.

That's a joke, of course, but then again, so are NBA refs. In large part, this isn't really their fault—basketball is a fast-moving game with fiddly rules, each of which can be interpreted in any number of different ways. But refs would do themselves and everyone else a favour if they stopped handing out so many fouls. Basketball is a sport with 'personal fouls' and 'team fouls', 'flagrant fouls' and 'technical fouls'. You can be charged for elbowing, blocking or charging. You can even be charged for breathing.

Don't believe me? One lunchtime in February 1998, the coach of the New York Point Park University team enjoyed an Italian meal chock-full of garlic. Come game time, it wasn't long before he took umbrage at a particular decision, and decided to share his thoughts with the ref.

His thoughts were fine but his breath was not. Technical foul.

Rhyme time

Steroids, hot pants, teddy bears, lubricant: some things really don't belong in a locker room. But chief among them is poetry. It may well be that 'the true poet is all the time a visionary', as WB Yeats put it, but he is never—repeat, *never*—a sportsman.

A basketball coach in Vermont forgot this basic truth way back in 1974. Butch Harmon decided that the best way to psyche up his boys before a big match would be to read out a poem called 'Don't Quit', and give each player his very own copy.

'After I read the poem, I asked each player his response to it,' Morgan later recalled. 'I took a few extra minutes to make sure each player had a chance to study the poem and talk about it. The gym was jammed and the fans were waiting for us to come out. The ref kept coming into the locker room and telling us to get out on the floor and I kept telling him we weren't done yet. I felt what I was doing in the locker room was more important than what was going to happen out on the court anyway.'

It wasn't. The team was penalised five points for coming out late on the court and ended up losing by one.

Einstein & Co.

'Nobody in football should be called a genius,' the NFL quarterback Joe Theismann once remarked. 'A genius is a guy like Norman Einstein.'

Basketball, on the other hand, is simply bursting with geniuses, as the following quotes help show.

- 'We went to a lot of clubs, but I can't remember if that was one of them.' Shaquille O'Neal, when asked if he visited the Acropolis while in Athens.

- 'Play some Picasso.' Chris Morris, to a piano player while trying to impress a date.

- 'He's one of the best power forwards of all time. I take my hands off to him.' Scottie Pippen.

- 'We're going to turn this team around 360 degrees.' Jason Kidd.

- 'My sister's expecting a baby, and I don't know if I'm going to be an uncle or an aunt.' Chuck Nevitt.

- 'Left hand, right hand, it doesn't matter. I'm amphibious.' Charles Shackleford.

- 'Any time Detroit scores more than 100 points and holds the other team below 100 points, they almost always win.' Doug Collins.

- 'Are you any relation to your brother Marv?' Leon Wood.

OLYMPIC
MOMENTS

At the Olympics in China, every colour was represented ... and that was just the drinking water.

Evan Sayet

The pride of Japan

Any idea who won the 1996 Olympic marathon in Atlanta?

Nope, me neither. But I can tell you who came last. Number 111 out of 111 runners, Abdul Baser Wasiqi of Afghanistan staggered into a closed stadium, empty of all but officials, a full 90 minutes behind runner 110. 'He walked quite a bit of the way, but he did jog across the finish line,' said an admiring fan. 'This is what the Olympics is all about.'

Impressive—but for true marathon-running greatness, there's no going past Japan's Shizo Kanakuri. His best time for the 26.2 mile course was a glorious 54 years, eight months, six days, eight hours, 32 minutes and 20 seconds. Starting out at the Stockholm Olympics of 1912, Kanakuri clocked up a steady ten or so miles but then began to feel a little parched. He spotted a family who were having a picnic, joined them for a drink, and then somehow drifted off to sleep. He woke up the next morning filled with shame—and meatballs—and hurriedly caught the next boat to Japan.

Five decades, six children and ten grandchildren later, however, Kanakuri was still filled with shame. So he returned to Stockholm to finish the race, and hobbled home for the honour of Japan.

McWhoops

McDonald's is famously good at marketing. The face and stomach of capitalism for well over 60 years, they're even now managing to persuade people that their burgers are a 'healthy choice'.

But the restaurant chain hasn't always been so savvy. In the 1960s, for example, Maccas actually made moves to ditch its iconic big M. The Golden Arches were only retained at the insistence of a design consultant and psychologist, who argued that they had a certain soothing, Freudian effect. Apparently the big M reminds our subconscious of 'Mother McDonald's nourishing breasts'.

Another marketing masterstroke came during the 1984 Los Angeles Olympics. With every purchase, the company announced, American customers would receive a scratch card with an Olympic event hidden on it. If the US won the event, the customer would win a prize. They got a Coke for a bronze medal, French fries for silver, and a Big Mac for gold.

The company's careful estimates of the amount of food they were going to have to give away were based on the US medal tally at the 1976 Montreal Olympics. But the communist bloc had competed at that Olympics and they chose to boycott the LA Games. In good news for patriots, but bad news for McMarketers, the lack of real competition meant that the US won a medal in practically every event.

'Would you like a new job with that?'

Faster, higher, stronger

Muhammad Ali always avoided sex for at least six weeks before a fight. During his boxing years, the elite athlete ate lightning, crapped thunder and avoided cuddle time at all costs.

But does avoiding sex make athletes perform better, so to speak? According to an Italian professor of endocrinology, sex actually *stimulates* the production of testosterone. 'After three months without sex, which is not so uncommon for some athletes, testosterone dramatically drops to levels close to children's levels.' For sports where 'a bit of extra aggression could be the difference' between winning and losing, the professor recommends 'complete and satisfactory sexual intercourse the evening before the game'.

Good to know. Perhaps jumping on the bandwagon of this brand-new science, organisers at the London Olympic Games in 2012 handed out 150,000 condoms to the athletes living in the Olympic village. Each and every athlete had more than 15 condoms at their disposal.

The science is still out on whether this was why so many world records were set.

Going for gold

The three medals awarded at the Olympics are supposed to represent Greek mythology's Three Ages of Man: the Golden Age, when men lived among the gods; the Silver Age, where youth lasted 100 years; and the Bronze Age, a time of heroes. They also represent a lot of hard work. Athletes train their whole lives to get to the Olympics and put one of those things around their neck. They get up early and they work until late. They compromise their relationships and they sacrifice other careers. Olympic glory involves blood, sweat, tears, pain and missing out on lots of excellent TV.

But apparently it becomes worth it when you first see that glint of gold. Soviet rower Vyacheslav Ivanov certainly seemed to feel that way when he won the single sculls at the 1956 Melbourne Games. Ecstatic, the 18-year-old tossed his gold medal up into the air.

It fell into the river and was never seen again.

Sportsmanship in Spain

The Paralympics have grown from a small gathering of British Second World War veterans in 1948 to one of the biggest sport events in the world. They're also one of the best. With the motto 'Spirit in motion', they can be a sight to stir the soul. They remind us that sport is not really about winning or losing—about being the fastest, the highest or the strongest. Sport is about overcoming challenges and being the best you can be.

That said, it's still nice to win. So there was something especially heart-warming about the Spanish basketball team at the Sydney Paralympics. It beat the Russian team 87–63 in the final of the intellectual disability tournament, taking home a coveted gold medal. 'There were two or three players . . . who could have competed in our national basketball league,' said one Australian coach. 'What they did with and without the ball was way above what any of our athletes could have achieved.'

Our hearts were less warm a little afterwards, however, when it emerged that ten of the 12 Spanish players hadn't actually been disabled at all.

Champagne comedy

Champagne and sport share a special relationship: the bubbly French wine represents the taste of victory. Each year in the final ceremonial leg of the Tour de France, the winning rider sips a glass while riding through the streets of Paris. And when the winners gather on the podium after each Formula One car race, a magnum of G.H. Mumm gets sprayed around.

But sometimes the taste can turn sour. In the 1908 London Games marathon, South African Charles Hefferon was coasting to victory. He was over a mile ahead of his nearest rival, with less than two miles left to run. Clearly this was no time for water! Suffering from a fatal combination of thirst and overconfidence, Hefferon accepted a small glass of champagne from a tipsy spectator.

It cost him the race. Hefferon collapsed, cramping and vomiting, less than a mile from the finish, and had to be stretchered away.

No angel

If you're the sort of person who likes to see blood spilt, the Olympics probably aren't your thing. Even its contact sports like karate and judo often seemed designed to avoid any contact at all. Watch an Olympic boxing match, for example, and you'll see two teenagers in big helmets daintily sparring as they dance cautiously around a ring. The winner is whoever accumulates the most points. If they actually hurt their opponent, they'd probably get sued.

Olympic taekwondo, similarly, could be shown on children's television without causing the slightest fuss. Any hint of an injury, and the authorities are quick to step in. In 2008, for example, a Cuban fighter named Angel Matos copped a glancing blow to the foot. The rules only allowed him a brief window of time to stop the bleeding, but—perhaps not realising this because of the language barrier—the injury wasn't bandaged up in time. Matos was disqualified, which made him *furious*.

What must have made it even more frustrating was the fact that his toe was absolutely fine. He proved this by kicking the referee in the face.

The Olympic spirit

'The most important thing in the Olympic Games is not to win but to take part, just as the most important thing in life is not the triumph but the struggle. The essential thing is not to have conquered but to have fought well.' So said Baron Pierre de Coubertin, the founder of the Modern Olympics and the owner of a really great moustache. For de Coubertin, the Olympics were about more than just sport; they were an avenue to world peace. What better way to remove prejudice than 'to bring the youth of all countries periodically together for amicable trials of muscular strength and agility?'

Stirring stuff in theory, but in practice you're dealing with people. Two people at the Paris 1900 Olympics, for example, were Meyer Prinstein and Alvin Kraenzlein. Those athletes were coming first and second in the long jump, with just one day to go. That day was a Sunday, however, so the two men agreed to stay away from the track, and devote the day to their Lord.

Or rather, one man did. Ever so quietly, Kraenzlein snuck out of church at the very last moment to take advantage of a huge tailwind. His final jump beat Prinstein's by a single centimetre, and put a gold medal around his neck.

He also got a black eye, after Prinstein gave him a punch in the face.

Stayin' power

With his lush, velvety baritone and oh-so-sensual lyrics, Barry White has been a successful love doctor for several million sex-starved couples. Put some of his butter-smooth soul on the stereo, and you'll have either sex or a damn good laugh. Good times either way.

Just don't play his music the night before a drug test. An American bronze medal-winning sprinter called Dennis Mitchell did just that in 1998. The fatal combination of 'I'm Qualified to Satisfy You' with 'Staying Power' and 'I'm Going to Love You Just a Little More, Baby' led him to make love to his wife five times.

So? Well, all this bedroom action created an unnaturally high level of testosterone in his body, which meant that he failed a drug test the next day. Mitchell spent the next two years banned from his sport—and probably vowed to ban Barry from the bedroom.

Boginskaya the bitch

The people who say sport is 'only a game' have never met Svetlana Boginskaya. The owner of three Olympic gold medals, this young Soviet gymnast of the 1970s was known to her fans as 'the Swan of Belarus'. Among acquaintances, she was known as a bitch.

'She was the most arrogant, most impossible person I ever saw,' says coach Bela Karolyi, a clear fan of straight talking. 'I thought she had a nasty personality. Everything I saw from her on the floor was bad—the way she treated people, the way she talked with coaches and team mates, the way she scared the athletes from other teams. I always thought she was an arrogant, ego-filled, very sad personality.'

True enough, but she was only a kid. 'When I first started gymnastics, I hated to see other girls who I thought were a little bit better than I was,' admits an older, wiser woman today. 'I used to bite them in the changing room after practice. I used to kick them and pull their hair until they cried.'

Luckily, however, the girls' mothers hit upon a solution. They started to bring Svetlana lollies and chocolates, on the condition that the violence ceased.

The plan half worked. 'I took the candy, but I'd keep doing it.'

BASEBALL
MOMENTS

Ninety percent of this game is half mental.

Yogi Berra

The demanding coach

If your idea of fun involves yelling at a roomful of people, making them do laps, and then yelling at them some more, a coaching career could be for you. Stories of super-demanding coaches abound in every sport. There are coaches who forbid sex and coaches who forbid smiles. Coaches who stick players in ice chambers and coaches who train them in deserts. Coaches who make players exercise until they vomit and coaches who make them exercise *while* they vomit.

And then there's Groucho Marx, the most demanding coach of all. During the 1950s, Hollywood's actors and comedians liked to have an annual baseball match to raise money for charity. Groucho was put in charge of the comedians one year, and he was quick to make his voice heard. 'All right, get up there and hit a home run,' he instructed his lead-off hitter, Jack Benny.

Benny stepped up to the plate and struck out.

So Groucho immediately resigned. 'I can't manage a team that won't follow instructions!'

Stan the man

'Stanley' is no name for a sportsman, but some talents won't be denied. Three-time MVP Stan 'the Man' Musial is one of baseball's all-time greats. Throughout a 22-year career with the St Louis Cardinals, Musial hit 475 home runs, won three World Series championships and broke an extraordinary 17 Major League records. Barack Obama recently presented him with the Presidential Medal of Freedom, the highest honour a US citizen can receive.

In other words, Stan could bat. Pitchers were naturally aware of this, so they put a lot of thought into the sorts of balls they should throw. Some tried sliders, others tried screwballs—and others thought about suicide, before giving a curveball a go.

In a 1951 All-Star game, a Yankee pitcher named Ed Lopat announced that he'd finally cracked it. 'Watch this,' he told his fellow pitcher, Preacher Roe. 'I know the perfect way to pitch against Musial.'

Lopat stepped up to the mound, unleashed his secret weapon—and watched helplessly as Stan hit a home run.

'I see what you mean,' yelled out Roe. 'But I found that way to pitch to him a long time ago, all by myself.'

Marvellous Marv

In the 1962 baseball season, beating the New York Mets was like shooting fish in a barrel. Extremely big fish, we should probably add, in a very small barrel. And for the metaphor to be really accurate, the fisherman would need a bazooka. In other words, the Mets were bad. Packed with has-beens, never-weres and cast-offs from other clubs, their 120 losses in that dire season made them poster boys for abject failure. Baseball experts agree that the 1962 Mets were the worst team to ever disgrace a field.

And Marv Throneberry was probably their worst player. Marv had been a reasonably capable first contributor in the minor leagues, but he was totally out of his depth at the top. He led the league in errors at first base in 1962, and his fielding percentage of 0.981 was the worst in baseball history.

One time, the story goes, the Mets' manager was presented with a cake on his birthday. A player asked why 'Marvellous' Marv, who'd turned 28 recently, hadn't got a cake for his.

'We were afraid he might drop it.'

Moving on

Professional athletes tend to become accustomed to stardom and a certain way of life. So retirement can hit them hard. They lose close contact with team mates and the adoration of the fans. It's not cancer, but it's not fun: post-career depression has struck Ashes stars and Olympic gold medallists, Grand Slam winners and world boxing champs.

Modern sports teams are increasingly aware of the problem, and are putting appropriate measures in place. In the AFL, for example, past players have access to counselling and career support, as well as first-class financial advice. Most of the clubs have past-players associations and mentoring opportunities to help ex-players still feel part of the team.

Things are a little different in Major League Baseball—or at least they were back in 1967. 'They broke it to me gently,' recalls Bob Uecker of his 'retirement' from the Atlanta Braves. 'The manager came up to me before a game and told me that they didn't allow visitors in the clubhouse.'

Babe and the kid

George 'Babe' Ruth was more than a big man: he was a big man with a big heart. Back in the summer of 1926, a baseball-mad little boy named Johnny Sylvester was kicked in the head by a horse. Bedridden for months, his condition gradually worsened. Doctors eventually diagnosed osteomyelitis, an infection that leads to bone deterioration and then, in most cases, death. Desperate to boost his spirits, the boy's family contacted his favourite sports team, the New York Yankees, and were rewarded with a baseball signed by the Babe. 'I'll knock a homer for you on Wednesday,' he wrote. And proceeded to knock not one, but three.

Then came the miracle: as was famously depicted in the film *The Babe Ruth Story*, little Johnny suddenly got well. Perhaps a home run really is the best medicine?

Less famous was another incident that occurred a few years later. It's said that one of Johnny's uncles happened to run into the Babe, and took the opportunity to assure him that the boy was still well. With tears in his eyes and a tremor in his voice, he thanked the champ with all of his heart.

'Glad to do it,' said the gracious Great Bambino. 'Send him my regards.'

But after the uncle left, Babe turned to a friend. 'Now, who the hell is Johnny Sylvester?'

Money, money, money

'I'm tired of hearing about money, money, money, money, money,' Shaquille O'Neal once complained. 'I just want to play the game, drink Pepsi and wear Reebok.'

If he'd played pro sport three or four decades ago, Big Shaq might have got his wish. The 1970s were a cleaner, purer time in sport, because there simply wasn't that much money about. Sportspeople had to play for the love of the game.

They also seemed to take their duties more seriously. 'To me, everyone who wears a uniform carries the responsibility of becoming a positive role model,' said former Philadelphia third baseman, Mike Schmidt. 'When I think about it, this is more important than any home run, any play, or any statistic. All these fade with time. But being a positive role model both on and off the field helps others become better human beings.'

Nice. But none of that means you can't also help yourself. In 1980, Philadelphia won the World Series, and held a big banquet to celebrate. 'What can I say about Mike Schmidt,' the team owner's speech began, 'now that he's been named Most Valuable Player for both the National League and the World Series?'

Schmidt's voice rang out from the crowd: 'Renegotiate!'

The chatty Yankee

Baseball catcher Lawrence 'Yogi' Berra was famous for never shutting up. The only thing that could ever stop him talking was the need to occasionally breathe. No batter could step up to the plate against the New York Yankees, therefore, without hearing a bit of Berra behind him.

'See any good movies lately?' he might ask the first baseman. 'How's the garden?' 'What's your favourite food?' The conversation might move on to the weather, or a detailed account of his last golf game.

'Can't you get that son of a bitch to shut up?' an exasperated batter once asked the umpire—perhaps after a friendly query about the state of his health.

'Well, if he's talking to you, he's not talking to me,' replied the umpire, who'd recently had to sit through an account of Berra's latest funny dream.

Another umpire took even more direct action. Whenever Berra stepped up to bat, he liked to ask the umpire how his family was.

'They died last night,' the umpire replied on one occasion. 'Get in there and hit.'

The story of Sidd Finch

One of the more depressing developments in world sports over recent years has been the decline in old-fashioned characters. It just takes so much discipline to be a professional athlete these days—so much dieting and training and stress—that there's little room for personality. Almost from childhood, the best of the best are 100% focussed on their quest, and act with a single-minded purpose and drive.

Still, every now and then, a genuine character *does* come along—and journalists rejoice as one. You could almost taste their excitement on 1 April 1985, after a new edition of *Sports Illustrated* came out. It seemed that an amazing new baseballer had appeared on the scene. 'He's a pitcher, part yogi and part recluse,' the article's tagline said. 'Impressively liberated from our opulent lifestyle, Sidd's deciding about yoga—and his future in baseball.'

The article told the amazing story of Sidd Finch, who could pitch an amazing 168 miles per hour—the world record was 103—without even needing a warm-up. A Harvard graduate who liked to play in one shoe, Sidd was a reluctant star: he wasn't interested in sport so much as his soul. Interested recruiters were advised to go to Tibet, where Sidd was currently studying the 'yogic mastery of mind-body' under the 'great poet-saint Lama Milaraspa'.

A week of intense public and media interest followed the article, and a number of recruiters swung into action.

Then it finally occurred to someone to examine the article's tagline. If you write out the first letters of all those words, they spell: 'Happy April Fool's Day—ah fib'.

Perfect practice

'Practice does not make perfect,' declared the great coach Vince Lombardi. '*Perfect* practice makes perfect.' Great sportspeople, in other words, don't just train hard, they train smart. Going the extra mile doesn't help that much if you're going in the wrong direction.

Sam Narron was not a smart trainer. In fact, he wasn't really smart, full stop. An underachieving catcher for the St Louis Cardinals, Narron once approached his coach, Frank Frisch, and asked for some advice as to how he should train. Easy, replied Frisch. Just pick out someone you admire and copy whatever they do.

For the next few hours, Frisch leaned on the batting cage, watching various sluggers go through their drills. He looked and looked but saw no Narron—then realised that the player was actually lying down, taking it easy, nearby.

'Didn't I tell you to pick out someone and copy him?'

'Yes, Mr Frisch, and I picked you.'

Classic catches

There are few finer sights in baseball than someone taking a spectacular catch. The best are the so-called 'home-run robbers'—catches that see an outfielder jump up to intercept a ball that will otherwise finish over the fence.

The gold standard in home-run robbing was set by a Milwaukee Brewers player named Ryan Braun. In perhaps the greatest catch in baseball history, he once prevented a certain homer by literally running up the left-field wall, doing a full 180-degree turn, and flicking the baseball back from above the fence with his outstretched glove. Braun then landed on the ground, neatly caught the ball and began celebrating in one smooth motion.

The brown standard, however, was set by a right-fielder named Jose Canseco. In 1993, a Cleveland Indians batter hit a fly ball that threatened to soar over the fence. As it happened, it was a little too low for that, but this turned out not to matter. An overenthusiastic Canseco misjudged his leap towards the wall and the ball bounced on his head—and over the fence. Home run.

Casey Stengel, talent spotter

It takes talent to spot talent—to know which teenagers will make the big time and which ones are a waste of time. Every sport is full of bright young hotshots who are all set to conquer the world—until they don't and become bitter old men.

In 1960s America, recruiting was more of an art. Baseball managers like Casey Stengel didn't rely on statistics so much as old-fashioned know-how, gut and hunch. Stengel was once asked about the future prospects of two promising 20-year-old baseballers called Ed Kranepool and Greg Goossen.

'In ten years,' he replied, 'Ed Kranepool has a chance to be a star. In ten years, the other guy has a chance to be 30.'

A disgrace to the game

Superstitions are a big part of sport, even among the best. Tiger Woods plays in a red shirt on Sundays and Bjorn Borg never shaved during Wimbledon. Wayne Gretzky would always tuck one side of his jumper into his pants, while Michael Jordan always wore a pair of shorts from his uni days underneath his Chicago Bulls shorts.

Ed Farber was not a superstar, but he had a superstition too: clean uniforms were bad luck. A mediocre shortstop who played in a series of mediocre baseball leagues, Farber was once drafted by the Montreal Royals, a team in the mediocre International League. On his first day at the Royals, he superstitiously took off his top, dropped it in some mud, and proceeded to rub, rub, rub.

'What on earth are you doing?' screamed his furious coach. 'You're a disgrace to the game. Go to the clubhouse at once, take off that uniform and burn it. I never want to see it again.'

Farber dutifully went to the clubhouse, and found some newspaper and matches. A while later, the coach went to find him—and discovered a blazing fire.

'Farber, a little while ago, I fired you and told you to burn your uniform. Well, you're hired again because you're the first player I ever saw in my life who did exactly what he was told to do.'

Big Babe's big wage

'No Congress of the United States ever assembled has met with a more pleasing prospect than that which appears at the present time,' declared President Calvin Coolidge in his annual State of the Union address. The year was 1927.

Two years later, the US was in the worst depression in the history of the world, and big Cal was out on his arse. But his replacement wasn't too much better. 'Gentleman, you have come sixty days too late. The Depression is over,' President Hoover told a delegation requesting immediate government action—in June 1930.

As the US braced itself for a decade's worth of economic disasters—a decade of homelessness, starvation and disease—one of life's few bright spots was the Babe. Far and away the best baseballer that ever lived, Babe Ruth put bums on seats and smiles on faces. But he didn't do it for free. At the height of the Depression, the Yankees asked their star if he could take a cut in his $80,000 salary. He refused.

'But that's more money than Hoover got for being president last year.'

'I know,' replied the Babe. 'But I had a better year.'

Lateral thinking

When you're recruiting the next generation of sports stars, you need to think outside the box. AFL recruiters, for example, sometimes sign up basketball players on the basis that their game requires similar physical attributes and not-too-dissimilar skills. American gridiron teams, in turn, have been known to recruit AFL stars as punters— punters being the players who actually kick the ball. Essentially, it comes down to vision. The athletes of tomorrow can be fat or skinny, unco or unfit, but it's a recruiter's job to look past all that and see something else—that special quality which makes the star.

The baseball manager Charlie Grimm provides a good example of this kind of lateral thinking. When Grimm was in charge of the Chicago Cubs, he once took a phone call from a talent scout who was convinced he'd struck baseball gold.

'Charlie, I've landed the greatest young pitcher in the land!' said the recruiter, excitedly. 'He struck out every man who came to bat—27 in a row. Nobody even got a foul until two were out in the ninth. The pitcher is right here with me. What shall I do?'

'Sign up the guy who got the foul. We're looking for hitters.'

Positive thinking

Professional sportspeople are always being instructed to give 100%—or 110% if their coach doesn't understand maths. They are told that they have to 'bring their A-game' and 'come to play'—that 'winners are grinners' and losing's 'gotta hurt'.

One pitcher for the New York Yankees, however, avoided clichés like the plague. In 1978, Richard 'Goose' Gossage cranked out a couple of spectacular pitches to give his team an unlikely win in the play-offs. Eager journalists everywhere wanted to know the secret of his success. Exactly what, they asked Goose breathlessly, went through his mind at the crucial moment?

'I was thinking that the worst thing that could happen if we lose is that, at this time tomorrow, I'll be skiing in the Rockies.'

Life with George

In the northern winter of 1973, an erratic shipping million-aire named George Steinbrenner bought the New York Yankees for $10 million. He was quick to reassure fans that he would not be active in the day-to-day operations of the club: 'I'll stick to building ships.'

He lied. While Steinbrenner's four decades at the Yankees was a time of extraordinary success, netting seven World Championships and 11 pennants, it was also a time of extraordinary chaos. The bombastic boss fired 20 coaches in his first 23 years, and employed 11 different general managers.

The players often incurred his wrath as well. 'It must be very disappointing when you lose games like you have been of late,' a journalist once asked pitcher Albert Lyle after the Yankees had been through a bad month.

'I don't know. It's not all bad.'

'What do you mean, not all bad?'

'Well, the more we lose, the more George becomes angry. And the more angry he becomes, the more he flies to watch us play. And the more he flies, the more chance there is that his plane will crash.'

The role model

One of the most heartening things about sport is that it can help people be their best. Growing up dirt-poor on the desolate plains of Ohio, William 'Gates' Brown didn't have the most promising start in life. A sports star at his local high school, he was constantly in and out of trouble. He was eventually sent to prison at 18 after being convicted of breaking and entering.

While inside Mansfield State Reformatory, however, the problem child got serious about baseball, was recruited by the Detroit Tigers, and went on to break the American League record for all-time pinch-hits in a career. These days, he's an excellent citizen—and a perfect role model for wayward kids.

Once upon a time, the Tigers star returned to his Ohio high school to see some of those kids in person. 'I'm sure some of our students would be interested to know,' gushed the principal in front of the assembly hall, 'what did you take when you were in school?'

'Overcoats, mostly.'

Wesley Branch Rickey

No one ever laughed at Wesley Branch Rickey—nope, not even when they heard his middle name. The tough, no-nonsense Major League Baseball executive was called 'sir' by his underlings (who probably included his wife and kids).

To his players, Rickey always stressed the moral and spiritual discipline the righteous man needed in life. 'Do you smoke, son?' he would grill them keenly. 'Do you run around with fast women? Do you drink?' To his hardworking employees, Rickey stressed the need for economy. His time was important and precious, he said, so never use two words when one would do.

On one occasion, he had his secretary wire an underling to ask whether they'd closed out a deal. 'Yes,' the underling duly replied.

By the time Rickey got around to reading the message, however, his secretary had gone—and so had his memory of the original question. Baffled, he wired back, 'Yes, what?'

'Yes, sir!' came the dutiful reply.

The Daffiness Boys

The Brooklyn Dodgers players of the early 20th century were not renowned for their intelligence. Affectionately known as the 'Daffiness Boys', the Dodgers became the laughing stock of professional baseball during the 1920s, thanks to a long series of stupid mistakes—think of Inspector Clouseau handcuffed and blindfolded playing baseball without knowing the rules.

Naturally, this made them a little frustrating to coach. The story goes that after one particularly daffy game, in which three of the lovably inept players somehow managed to end up on third base at the exact same time, the manager announced that the next man who did anything stupid would be given a $10 fine.

He then stormed out of the dugout to present the umpire with the team batting order and handed him a laundry slip instead.

The bartender and Babe Ruth

Baseball has many amazing true stories – but the made-up ones are more fun. Take this classic about a man and a dog who walked into a bar, right past a sign saying 'No dogs allowed'.

'Get out, pal' growled the thickset, tattooed bartender, gesturing to the sign with a meaty fist.

'But this is a special dog,' the man said undaunted. 'He can speak English, just you watch. Fido,' he went on, after a theatrical pause, 'what is on top of this building?'

'Roooof' his furry companion replied.

'And how does sandpaper feel?'

'Ruuuuff.'

'See, isn't that amazing!' asked the dog-owner triumphantly – only to be a little discouraged by the bartender's scowl. 'Ok, ok, give us one more chance. Fido, who's the greatest baseballer of all time.'

Fido paused for a few moments, seeming almost thoughtful. Then he finally let forth with a confident 'Roooth'.

'Right, that's it,' said the bartender, his patience at an end. He grabbed the man by his shoulders and the dog by its ears and frogmarched both to the footpath outside. And there they stood for the next little while, feeling more than a little sheepish.

'What should I have said?' the dog asked eventually. 'Joe DiMaggio?'

Baseball at Harvard

Why do most people like sport? More academics than you might expect have turned their mind to this question, and their answers generally cite evolution. At a biological level, the argument goes, sports remind us of the thrill of the hunt—the excitement of being a predator or the thrill of being prey.

Or not. Anyway, to my mind, a more interesting question is why do some people *not* like sport? What's wrong with them and can it be cured? One of the best examples of this strange psychological phenomenon came in the form of Charles William Eliot, a distinguished professor of mathematics and chemistry who was president of Harvard University for 40 years. A smart man in many ways, but completely stupid in another.

One year, after Harvard's baseball team had taken all before it in the Ivy League, Eliot announced entirely out of the blue that he was thinking of banning the sport.

'Well, this year I'm told the team did well because one pitcher had a fine curve ball. I understand that a curve ball is thrown with a deliberate attempt to deceive. Surely that is not an ability we should want to foster at Harvard?'

Manly Marty

Baseball isn't softball. To play it, you have to be hard. Take Hughie Jennings, a Major League batter who was hit by almost 300 pitches throughout his career, most of them in the head. But he just kept on keeping on. One time, after a particularly nasty hit, Hughie calmly insisted on finishing the game, and when it was finished, he fell into a three-day coma.

Another man's man was Josias Manzanillo, a relief pitcher for the Seattle Mariners. In 1997, one of his pitches was hit straight back at him, smack bang in the groin—where it crushed a testicle. But before he was rushed to hospital, where doctors ended up removing said goolie, Josias found time to throw out a batter who would have otherwise got a home run. You've got to admit, that takes a lot of ball.

What a pair of tough guys. An outfielder for Baltimore Orioles may well belong in their exalted company. Or he may not—you decide. In 2002, a freak accident meant Marty Cordova sustained severe burns all over his body and was forced to miss several games. He'd fallen asleep in a tanning bed.

MISCELLANEOUS MOMENTS

We had a good team on paper. Unfortunately,
the game was played on grass.

Brian Clough

MISCELLANEOUS MOMENTS

We had a good team... on paper. Unfortunately,
the game was played on grass.

Brian Clough

The killer instinct

A scene in the movie *Airplane* sees a stewardess hand out reading material before a flight. 'Do you have something light?' a passenger asks her. 'Well, how about this leaflet?' she answers. *'Famous Jewish Sports Legends.'*

If the writer of that leaflet needed more material, they should have included this story from Rebbe Nachman. A few hundred years ago, the rabbi wrote, the Russian army liked to recruit new soldiers by some rather unsavoury means. Essentially, their method involved finding some likely young men and clunking them on the head. When they woke up, they were soldiers.

One day, the army did this with a bunch of rabbis. Waking up in training camp in Siberia, these young rabbis were given bows and arrows—and mastered the weapon in the blink of an eye. To a man, they were all sharpshooters, so when it came time for battle, they got put in the front line.

As the enemy charged, an officer gave the order: 'Ready! Aim! *Fire!*'

No reaction.

'Fire!' he repeated. 'I order you to fire!'

Nothing.

'Excuse me, sir,' said one of the rabbis. 'Perhaps you cannot see. There are people in the way.'

Andre the giant alcoholic

'It takes only one drink to get me drunk,' George Burns once admitted. 'The trouble is, I can't remember if it's the 13th or the 14th.'

With Andre the Giant, it was about the 50th. That World Wrestling Federation wrestler stood seven feet, four inches tall thanks to acromegaly—a gland condition that leads to extra growth hormones—but it was his drinking that really soared to the heights. Said to consume over 7000 calories of alcohol a day, Andre once drank 41 litres of beer in six hours. On another occasion, he drank 16 bottles of wine in four hours—then got into the ring and won three fights.

But drinking before battle doesn't always work. It's said Andre once drank two cases of beer before a six-man tag-team fight, in which his opponent was Bad News Allen. For Allen, this was bad news indeed. Once he'd got his opponent on the floor, Andre sat on his face, as wrestlers often do. Then he lost control of his bowels, as wrestlers generally don't.

The fight ended up being cancelled. A technical—and rather smelly—draw.

Award-losing journalism

Most journalists are like human bloodhounds, absolutely relentless in their quest for the truth. There's no place to hide when they're hunting down a story, no way to mask the scent of a scoop. Or so we're told, anyway. Some students at the University of Akron may have gotten a slightly different impression in the 1970s, when they submitted a fake story to their local paper as a joke. Published word for word in *The Buchtelite*, their article made out that they were members of the university's (non-existent) ping-pong team, and had been winning a few games of late.

'The first article was real small,' recalled ringleader Jim Stein. 'We were half scared that people would figure out it was fake . . . but they picked it up and printed it word for word. Then the next week, we became more emboldened.'

Several articles later, they'd become very emboldened: a 41-inch article congratulated the team on winning an entirely fictional championship. 'By the time that came out, I'd say half the campus knew that it was a hoax. Everybody but *The Buchtelite* staff.'

A great gag, with only one downside: the byline of one of the paper's sports reporters often appeared on the stories. 'That infuriated us,' says Stein. 'They were plagiarising our fake articles!'

On the road

It would be wrong to say that 80s wrestlers looked like transvestites. This is because the politically correct term is 'transgendered'.

When this sport for long-haired, heavily made-up, semi-nude people was at its most flamboyant, two of its better practitioners were Ric Flair and the cowboy-hat wearing Blackjack Mulligan. The story goes that the boys were driving south—in full make-up and costumes—to ply their trade one day, when they asked their manager to stop the car. It was a stiflingly hot afternoon and they'd had lots of beers, so they needed to take a leak.

The manager had a sense of humour, however, so when they were safely out of sight behind a tree, he slowly drove away. What made this funny was that Ric Flair was barefoot and the road was boilingly hot, so he was forced to hop on Blackjack's back, as they chased down the car.

Reunited with the car a little later, all three men were listening to the radio as a truck driver with a story called in. He'd just seen a cowboy chasing a car, he reported, while carrying the ugliest woman the driver had ever seen on his back.

Bulls and balls

Bullfighting is a pretty despicable sport, but it does at least require some courage. For one thing, matadors have to dress up in capes, tights and sequins. For another, they often get killed. The bull, lest we forget, will *always* get killed, and generally in a pretty gruesome manner—but the last few centuries have seen almost 300 matadors get killed alongside them, together with over 200 banderilleros and picadors. On top of that they risk all sorts of injuries, from pierced thighs and ruptured rectums, to gored groins and broken backs. An angry bull is like a runaway train: best avoid it, if you can.

A matador named Christian Hernandez probably agrees with me. In 2010, the 22-year-old was the darling of Mexico City when he stepped out in pink tights to face a 400 kilogram bull. Then he took a quick step back. Abruptly deciding that he'd rather face the exit, Hernandez spun around and ran away as quickly as he could.

'I felt a deep fear, and I decided no, no, and no,' he later confessed. 'There are some things you must be aware of about yourself. I didn't have the ability. I didn't have the balls. This is not my thing.'

Ugly parents

'Ugly parent syndrome' is a feature of most kids' sports. Most of us have seen a few of these mums and dads on the sidelines, loudly instructing their little darlings to 'lift their bloody game'. 'For Christ's sake Sammy, kick the darn thing!' they will yell at a footy match. 'Catch that bitch!' they will tell ten-year-old Daisy. 'Pull out her ringlets and scratch her face!'

Some ugly parents, however, are even uglier than that. Take a Texan mum called Wanda Webb Holloway. Her daughter Shanna wanted to be a high school cheerleader, but couldn't quite make the team. Wanda stepped up her gruelling training regime, forcing Shanna to practise through injuries and illness, but it was all to no avail. Every time there was an audition, a neighbour's daughter would edge Shanna out.

If at first you don't succeed, someone has to die. Wanda's next move was to hire a hitman to kill the neighbour. She reasoned that the daughter would probably be so upset she'd no longer want to cheer. The plot was foiled and Wanda went to jail—and, alas, Shanna never made the team.

A thrill for the kids

Raelene Boyle is a seven-time Commonwealth gold medallist, whose three Olympic silvers (behind East German drug cheats) should in all fairness be counted as gold. She is one of Australia's greatest ever track and field athletes: a sprinter of rare grace and power who made a career out of overcoming odds.

But for some people that isn't enough. Back in 1980, Boyle's nieces begged their celebrity aunt to pay a visit to their little school in Brisbane because 'no one believed them when they said I was their aunt'. Dutifully, the sprinter came by one day, and 'was overwhelmed with the greeting I received as I was taken to each class. The children were very thrilled to meet me and each class had several questions to ask me.

'But I was brought back to earth in the preparatory unit. One little fellow was not at all impressed with my track record. He stood up and asked me in a deep, rough voice: "But can you swim?"'

The Swiss Miss

Martina Hingis won five Grand Slam singles titles during her tennis career, but she didn't win too many hearts. Great forehand, yes. Great backhand, certainly. But her personality was a D-minus at best.

Don't believe me? Meet Martina:

- 'People say that I am arrogant. But I am number one in the world so I have a right to be arrogant!'
- 'I'm glad you're doing this story on us and not on the WNBA. We're so much prettier than all the other women in sports.'
- 'What rivalry? I win all the matches.'
- 'She was trying hard, like she actually had a chance.'
- 'Sometimes I feel, I've been there, done it, now what? What more is there to prove?'
- 'It's all the time, "Tiger Woods, Tiger Woods." I am better than he is. I've been on top longer and I am younger. I'm just better.'

A rather more popular Swiss tennis player is, of course, Roger Federer. When the Fed Express won his first Wimbledon, way back in 2003, his compatriots were so excited, they gave him a cow. In a traditional ceremony in Gstaad, Fed was formally presented with the 800 kilogram beast and asked what he'd like to call it.

Onlookers began to shout out suggestions. 'Martina' was the most popular.

Stating the non-obvious

Judge people by what they do, not by what they say, is a lesson I always got from my parents. It is hard to do this with sports commentators.

- 'I am a firm believer that if you score one goal, the other team have to score two to win.' Howard Wilkinson, soccer commentator.
- 'This is really a lovely horse. I once rode her mother.' Ted Walsh, horse racing commentator.
- 'Ah, isn't that nice. The wife of the Cambridge president is kissing the Cox of the Oxford crew.' Harry Carpenter, rowing commentator.
- 'Strangely, in slow motion replay, the ball seems to hang in the air for even longer.' David Acfield, cricket commentator.
- 'The lead car is absolutely, truly unique, except for the one behind it, which is exactly identical to the one in front of the similar one in back.' Murray Walker, Grand Prix commentator.
- 'Sure, there have been deaths in boxing but none of them serious.' Alan Minter, boxing commentator.
- 'And this is Gregoriava from Bulgaria. I saw her snatch this morning and it was amazing!' Pat Glenn, weightlifting commentator.
- 'Andrew Mehrtens loves it when Darryl Gibson comes inside of him.' Murray Mexted, rugby commentator.

Stand by your man

Behind every great man there's a great woman—and generally one who's a little surprised. The world of sport is packed with supportive girlfriends, helpful wives and obliging mums—women who do whatever it takes to help their man realise his dreams.

Take Victoria Beckham, for example. She helps husband, David, keep it real. The former Spice Girl was once quoted as saying that she and Becks have 'so many wider interests . . . fashion, make-up. I mean you think, yeah, football's great, and singing's great. But you've got to look at the bigger picture.'

Then there's Winifred Palmer, a women who took care of the little things. 'One of the reasons [golfer] Arnie Palmer is playing so well at the moment,' a commentator once noted, 'is that, before each final round, his wife takes out his balls and kisses them—Oh my God, what have I just said?'

But my favourite sporting spouse is Benedicte Tarango, the long-time wife of Jeff. A tennis player much like John McEnroe—except he wasn't that good—the notoriously feisty Tarango once served an ace that the umpire declared was a fault.

'You are the most corrupt official in the game!' Tarango screamed, storming off the court and refusing to play. Anxious to do her bit, Benedicte subsequently strode up to the official as he made his way back to the locker room and gave him a meaty slap in the face.

An unsafe bet

Some folks have the happy knack of being able to do something that other people are prepared to bet that they can't. It's said that one such man was Will Lovett. After the English snooker player somehow discovered that his mouth was big enough to accommodate a snooker ball, he struck upon a system where he bet strangers a beer that he could fit one in his mouth. Nights at the pub suddenly became very cheap.

But a good system means nothing if you're surrounded by bad people. After a few months of free beer, one of Will's buddies decided to secretly replace the regular snooker balls with some special ones that were a little oversized. After Will made a bet with the first sucker of the evening, he still amazingly managed to get one of the oversized balls in his mouth.

Getting it out took longer. Will suffered ripped lips and broken teeth, before being taken to hospital to get the ball removed by a surgeon.

Sexism in sport

Some sports are entirely free of sexual discrimination. These are the ones that women don't play. Sports like Formula One will be free of it forever, if Jenson Button has anything to do with the matter. There should never be women drivers, that F1 driver once said, because 'one week of the month you wouldn't want to be on the circuit with them, would you?' Also, 'a girl with big boobs would never be comfortable in the car. And the mechanics wouldn't concentrate. Could you imagine strapping her in?'

Tennis, sadly, is a different story. All too many male players appear to look down on their female colleagues, and despise the kind of game that they play. Pat Cash spoke for many when he said that 'women's tennis is two sets of rubbish that lasts only half an hour'.

But even there things could be changing. Sure, players still make sexist comments from time to time, but so intense is the public outrage, they then have to humbly retract. Take the kerfuffle that came when Wimbledon champ Richard Krajicek said that '80% of the top 100 women are fat pigs'.

After the ensuing media storm, the shamefaced Dutchman had to backtrack at a press conference: 'What I meant to say was that only 75% are fat pigs.'

The Devil's Favourite Demon

You should never judge by appearances, our parents always told us. But what if someone appears to be 'psychotic, demented, extremely violent, twisted, disturbed, unstoppable, isolated and at peace with insanity'?

That's how Wikipedia describes Kane. A seven foot, 147 kilogram wrestler who sports long dark hair, a blood-red mask and thigh-high black leather boots, Kane is the half-brother of the Undertaker and was horribly burnt in a fire as a child. Sometimes called 'The Devil's Favourite Demon', his signature moves include the 'big boot', the 'throat-thrust' and the 'power bomb'. He is the face—and tight black leotard—of death.

Kane does know the meaning of fear, however: he has passionate and devoted fans and he hates being harassed by them. Whenever his fights finish, he jumps straight in his car—still in his costume—and hurries back to his hotel before the public have a chance to bother him.

On one such occasion, it's said, he grabbed his key from the concierge and went straight up to his room for a shower—only to come face to blood-red face with an elderly couple, clutching each other and shivering with fear in his bed.

'I'm so sorry,' said the concierge a little while later. 'I gave you the wrong key.'

Andre and the hairpiece

When played at the highest level, sport requires 100% focus and concentration. Let your attention wander just for a moment, and all can very easily be lost. Andre Agassi may just have neglected this rule during his first ever Grand Slam final in 1990. Vain and balding, he had started wearing a wig in the late 1980s, both on court and in the shower. But the night before the final, as Agassi stood under the shower, he realised his wig was falling apart.

Panicking, he had his brother clamp it back on with hair clips: 'Do you think it will hold?'

'Just don't move so much.'

Of course Agassi could have played without the wig, but then he'd have had to deal with the reaction of the media, his opponents—and his fans. What would they say if they knew the handsome young player wore a wig?

'During the warming-up training before play I prayed,' Agassi recalled many years later. 'Not for victory, but that my hairpiece would not fall off. With each leap, I imagined it falling into the sand. I imagined millions of spectators move closer to their TV sets, their eyes widening and, in dozens of dialects and languages, ask how Andre Agassi's hair has fallen from his head.'

Perhaps this goes without saying, but I'll say it anyway: He lost.

Life in the public eye

When you're playing or coaching a professional sport, the media pressure can be intense. As an ever-growing number of journalists struggle to capture our ever-shrinking attention spans, coverage is getting more and more sensationalist, and intruding more and more into private lives.

Having said that, it can also be fun. An interview with a big magazine can be exciting, especially when you're still new to fame. The former basketball coach William 'Speedy' Morris is one of few men prepared to admit this. 'When I first got the job at La Salle,' he later recalled with a smile, 'the phone rang and my wife told me it was *Sports Illustrated*. I cut myself shaving and fell down the steps in my rush to get to the phone.

'When I got there, a voice on the other end said, "For just 75c an issue . . ."'

Three Dicks

Some sportspeople have great names. 'Shaq' is stylish and 'Tiger' is menacing. Usain Bolt says power, WG Grace says, well, grace.

Other sportspeople, however, do not have great names. Take the former Major League baseballer Dick Pole, for example, or his NFL colleague Dick Butkus. A couple of other well-known American footballers are Harry Colon and Craphonso Thorpe—though better known than either of them, ironically enough, was a Miami Dolphins player named Richie Incognito.

Another Richard is the NASCAR champ Dick Trickle, while an athlete who may also make you think 'STD' is the US swimmer, Misty Hyman. As a gold medallist, she did rather better at the Olympics than an also-ran South Korean pole vaulter named Kim Yoo Suk.

But for all the rugby union players named Danny Grewcock, or Australian goalkeepers named Norman Conquest, the names that most scare commentators are the ones like Prapawadee Jaroenrattanatarakoon, the ones that—without a *lot* of practice—are utterly unpronounceable.

Tom Nissalke fell into that category. Someone once asked that former coach of the Houston Rockets exactly how he pronounced his name.

'Tom,' was his reply.

No lack of members

Australians, as has been well-documented, *really* love their sport. But is it possible to love sport a bit too much? Take the story of a rowing race between a highly regarded Aussie bushman and the Canadian world champion on 22 May 1884. The interest in this race was so intense that an MP in the Victorian Parliament even suggested that an important vote should be postponed until the following day, to give all the pollies a chance to watch.

One of his fellow MPs was shocked. 'I trust the House will not accede to this suggestion?' thundered the self-righteous Mr Stuart. 'With the enormous amount of highly important work which we have before us, it would not be creditable to us as a legislative body to adjourn for the purpose of attending a boat race. I feel sure there will be no lack of members to form a quorum.'

He was wrong. They all went to the race.

(N)ever the diplomat

An article of faith for all sportspeople these days is 'always respect your opponent'. You may think that they're absolutely hopeless, you may be sure that you're going to win. But when a journalist asks you the question, 'I'm expecting a tough contest' is the only reply.

Unless you're Norma Plummer. The coach of our national netball team until 2011, Plummer took a fun and refreshing approach to sports psychology the day a journalist asked her about Australia's arch rival. New Zealand's national team, the Silver Ferns, were 'just a bunch of scrubbers,' she said.

'It was totally off the record and the next thing it was front page. You learn never to trust the media,' Plummer later told the, um, media.

'My daughter rang me up and she said, "Oh Mum, why did you say that?" I said, "What's wrong with that? It's just saying you're playing the bottom team".

'She did say it means something different these days.'

Losing the mind game

The great appeal of swimming is that it's so very simple. Some Hindu and Buddhist types even see it as a form of meditation. When you're doing laps, after all, you're alone and silent and apart from the world, while you breathe steadily and stare at the floor. Meanwhile, your whole body is weightless and focussed on one single objective, while your mind is free to drift where it likes. What could be more yoga than that?

The problem, of course, is that some people's minds drift a bit too far. In 2001, for example, Australia's women's 200-metre relay team was far and away the best in the world. It seemed that all Petria Thomas, Giaan Rooney, Elka Graham and Linda Mackenzie really had to do was swim straight, and the gold medal would be theirs for sure.

Fortunately, they did swim straight. Team anchor Rooney touched the wall first for a win. Unfortunately, they didn't *think* straight: urged on by a cameraman, the other three swimmers jumped into the pool to celebrate with Rooney . . . before all the other teams had finished.

Result? Disqualification.

Walter's whack

Walter Lindrum was a child prodigy. Far and away Australia's best ever billiards player, he was born into a family of snooker champions, and outstripped them all in his teens. This even though he'd lost half a finger in an accident as a three-year-old, and so had to learn how to play left-handed.

But Walter's success wasn't just due to talent: he also had to work, work, work. Standing on a crate so he could lean over the table, the young schoolboy practised for up to 12 hours a day.

Which didn't leave much time for school. Walter would often skip class to watch professional players ply their trade at a local snooker club—and there came a time when he was caught in the act. A teacher gave the future world champ six whacks with a cane and made him write 'billiards' 3500 times.

A couple of decades later, however, Lindrum dealt out a whack of his own. Playing at an exhibition match, he hit a ball off the table, which flew towards a spectator and bruised his knee. After the match, the spectator introduced himself. Surprise, surprise, it was Walter's old teacher.

'Remember me?'

'Remember you? What do you think I whacked you on the knee for?'

Knickerbocker glory

Every four years the Olympics roll around, and complaints about uniforms are quick to follow. While Australia's sportsmen mostly wear shorts and baggy t-shirts, you see, our sportswomen tend to get bra tops and bikini bottoms—or, if they're lucky, some tight green lycra. A recent Senate inquiry even found that many teenage girls abandon organised sport because of the uniforms they're forced to wear.

Things were very different back in 1908, when a Melbourne lady publicly declared that she would race any female over any distance for gate money and 'the title of champion woman runner of Australia'. The media outrage was intense. For a lady to become a professional athlete was scandalous enough, of course, but even worse was what she intended to wear. No bonnet, no corset, no blouse and no bustle. Just a full-length knickerbocker suit!

All right-thinking Melbournians vowed to stay away from this tawdry contest. So only several thousand people turned up to watch.